The Burns

The Burns Boys

Alistair Renwick

Cualann Press

ISBN 0 9544416 2 1

First Edition Autumn 2003

British Library Cataloguing in Publication Data. A catalogue record of this book is available at the British Library.

Published by
Cualann Press Limited
6 Corpach Drive
Dunfermline
KY12 7XG
Scotland
Tel/Fax 01383 733724
Email: cualann@btinternet.com
Website: www.cualann-scottish-books.co.uk

Printed by Bell & Bain, Glasgow

Acknowledgements

I thank Dr Peter Kedit, sometime Director of the Sarawak Museum, for his interest and insights into the history of his country from an Iban standpoint. I am also indebted to the National Library of Malaysia; the Library of Sarawak Museum; the State and British Council Libraries at Kuching; the History Centre and the Language and Literature Bureau of Brunei Darussalam for unstinted help. As the search intensified, I was granted frequent access to the Library of the National University of Singapore; the National Archives of that Republic and the *Straits Times* Library; I am most grateful. It is a particular pleasure to acknowledge an unknown librarian in the new town of Tampines, who suggested my last visit to the National Archives, where I chanced upon the letter from Matthew Burns.

In Scotland, many searched on my behalf and I thank the Carnegie Library, Ayr; Dunfermline Central Library and the Mitchell Library, Glasgow, where Mrs Janet McLaughlin and her colleagues kindly accommodated me on two visits of several days' duration, despite staff shortages. The National Library of Scotland and Edinburgh City Library were also helpful and I owe much to those Librarians in the Scottish Universities: Aberdeen (Special Collections and Archives); Edinburgh (Special Collections); Glasgow (Archives and Business Records Centre); St Andrews and Strathclyde. Mr James Crichton, Clerk of the Presbytery of Ayr, Mr Iain Milne, Librarian of the Royal College of Physicians of Edinburgh, Miss Alison Stevenson, Archivist of the Royal College of Surgeons of that city and Mr James Beaton, Librarian of the Royal College of Physicians and Surgeons, Glasgow, were most generous in response to my letters. England, too, holds valuable records that relate to Burns's murder and its aftermath and I thank those Librarians, Archivists and Curators at the following places: the University of Oxford; Brighton Library; the British Library (Social Policy Information Service; Newspaper Library and the Oriental and India Office Collections); the Library of the British Medical Association; the Guildhall Library, City of London; the General Register Office (England and Wales); Islington Reference Library; Liverpool Shipwreck and Humane Society; Lloyd's of London; London Metropolitan Archives; the Maritime Information Centre of the National Maritime Museum, Greenwich; the National Army Museum, London; the Public Information Office; the Public Records Office; Rhodes House Library, Oxford; the Record Office, the House of Lords; the Royal Commission on Historical Manuscripts, London; the Royal Pharmaceutical Society of Great Britain; the Wellcome Institute for the History of Medicine; the Worshipful

Society of Apothecaries and the University of Durham.

Specific genealogical questions were kindly answered by Mr Lawrence Burness, former Keeper of the William Coull Anderson Library of Genealogy, Arbroath, Scotland, and I acknowledge his early and sustained interest in this account. I am also indebted to Miss Paolozzi and her colleagues in the General Register Office for Scotland for their assistance and to the Scottish Record Office, as well as the Ulster Historical Foundation, Belfast, and the General Register Office in that city.

The discovery of Matthew Burns's letter in Singapore focused interest on what were then Oregon and Washington Territories in the Pacific Northwest of the United States, and much preliminary investigation was conducted by Internet, without which the task would have been more protracted. I thank Mrs Maxine Day Alexander; Mr Donald Crawford; Dr Tom Douglas; Mr Ray Edgar; Mr Stephen Greenberg, History of Medicine Division, National Library of Medicine; Mr Doug Jackman; Mr Philip Lothyan; Mr Frank McLean; Mr Egan Rand; Ms Jo Ann Wuitschick and Ms Kathy Zehner for their responses.

The bulk of the information on Matthew Burns is to be found in Washington State Archives and the State Library at Olympia. Here, Mrs Rebecca Christie, and Mr Terence Badger, Assistant State Archivist and their colleagues, were untiring in their help. Mr Mark Fox, Archivist, at the Department of Health in that state and the Registrar of the Royal College of Physicians and Surgeons of British Columbia also supplied useful information. I was greatly helped by the staff at Seattle Library, by Mr Tim Backer and Mr Abden Moberg of Oregon State Archives and Library, respectively, and by the National Archives and Records Administration, Pacific Region and Washington, D.C.

Dr Neil Renwick kindly found *De brieven van De Schoolmeester* in Amsterdam and I am much indebted to Associate Professor Kees Snoek, formerly of the University of Auckland, for his translations of parts of this book. Ms Penny Dempsey of the Australian National Maritime Museum, supplied information on the wreck of the *Princess Royal*. The penultimate draft was read by Mrs Catriona Renwick, Professor James Lawrie, Dr G. K. and Mrs Lotte Scott and Lindsay Renwick, all of whom suggested beneficial changes to the text. Mr Peter Jenkins kindly took the photograph of the Evans-Velge family memorial and Ms Yen Ho Suet drew the sketch maps and developed an idea for the cover from Kayan designs.

In conclusion, I thank the staff of the University of Auckland Library for their considerable help and Ms Sue Buglass, my former secretary, for her tireless efforts in processing the manuscript under less than ideal conditions. Bríd Hetherington receives the final accolade for fulfilling the writer's ambition of publication in Scotland.

Contents

Illustrations

Preface

Retirement brought an impelling need to strike out in other directions, so I accepted an invitation to work in Malaysia where, as a resident, I was able to indulge a penchant for local history. *The Pirate Wind* was an early purchase. First published in 1930, this account of the marauders of the South China Sea in particular, was written by Owen Rutter, sometime Magistrate and District Officer in British North Borneo.

Chapter XX, entitled *Murdered at Borneo*, describes the fate of Robert Burns, a grandson of the Scots poet, at the hands of Illanun pirates in 1851. I was at once intrigued, and vaguely recalled an article on the topic which appeared in *The Scots Magazine* some twenty years before my arrival in South-East Asia. A search of the new State Library in Kuala Lumpur confirmed several of Rutter's observations, but there were no official records and no primary sources of information.

In August 1994, I visited Kuching, the capital of Sarawak, where I was privileged to meet Dr Peter Kedit, then Director of the renowned Sarawak Museum. Besides summarising the history of the Brooke dynasty from an Iban standpoint, Dr Kedit gave me a rare off-print of a piece published in the Museum's journal by a predecessor, Tom Harrisson, to mark the centenary of Burns's death. This courageous Scot seemed worthy of fuller recognition in his native country and being a fellow-countryman, I resolved to explore the topic further, in the hope that a short article might meet this end. But as new evidence emerged *The Burns Boys* evolved into its present form.

Wherever possible I sought original documents but few have survived deleterious climates or the depredations of war, civil unrest and the dissolution of colonial rule. However, research in Singapore was a revelation. The Republic has wonderfully preserved its colonial past since its foundation by Stamford Raffles in 1819 and much new knowledge came to hand. The chance discovery of one letter in the National Archives led to largely unpublished sources in Washington State and, at their greatest extent, the ramifications of this story embraced South-East Asia, the United Kingdom and the United States.

I have tried to permit the protagonists to speak for themselves from documents, letters and publications of the period. I have also refrained from employing uniform spellings, of place-names in particular; for example, the Bruni of one writer is the Bruné of another. While this may exasperate some readers, all quotations are verbatim. On completion of what I considered the penultimate draft, I was disappointed. The history was accurate but dull and Borneo, its peoples and explorers are far from prosaic, so I contrived imaginary conversations in situations that were indeed real.

Lastly, in contrast to biographies of the giants of nineteenth-century exploration, this book tells only of exceptional interludes in the lives of two unexceptional men.

Introduction

There were no rituals. The perahu pointed nor'east in the offshore breeze and the corpses, like sacks, were heaved over the side. For a time, the four floated half-submerged in the warm water, the woman's hair spreading like fronds of black seaweed. The gentle lapping of the wavelets gradually dissolved the veneer of dried blood that ensheathed the cadavers and the crew's last sighting was of the European, distinguished in death by his pallor. Beneath him in the blue-green depths lurked the predators, roused from their torpor by the crimson ooze from savage wounds.

Chapter I

Glasgow

'Oh, come on, Matthew! Come on! The sodgers are comin'!' The younger boy, heartened by the crescendo of the side-drums, wiped tears and snot on his torn sleeve, rubbed a bleeding knee and ran to join his brother. Oblivious to cuffs and curses, they jostled and wormed their way to the front of the throng and cheered their heroes until the last rank faded from view. The crowd gradually dispersed and little huddles of weeping women and children were ingested by the mouths of dank closes that stank of urine. The streets fell silent and spurred by the fading light, the Burns boys quickened their pace as they marched along the granite setts to their home, a draper's shop on the south side of the Clyde. They were still singing 'We saw the Forty-Second/We saw them gang awa' as they burst into the kitchen at the back of the shop, where they were sharply rebuked by their sister. 'Wheesht, laddies, wheesht, ye'll waken the bairn!' So they sat by the fire and lulled by the warmth from the grate and the gentle bubbling of the soot-encrusted kail-pot on the hob, they fell asleep.

In Robbie's dream, the blue smoke that curled lazily up the lum was soon enveloped by the black reek from the steamboats on the river and towering above them, the tall masts of East Indiamen pierced the clouds. Newly arrived from the sub-continent and beyond, these leviathans bore wonderfully exotic cargoes and tales of strange lands and alien cultures. Before being roused for supper, Robbie saw himself as a young man bound for Eastern seas. His destiny had been revealed.

The draper hailed from Northern Ireland and in common with thousands of his countrymen, he emigrated to Glasgow in search of work. There he contrived to support his wife and family, but the added responsibility of his young brothers-in-law sorely taxed his inadequate income and Robbie left school before his thirteenth birthday to learn the trade. For ten to twelve hours each day, six days a week, he worked in the shop situated on the ground floor of a four-storeyed stone-built tenement that was close to one hundred years old.

The family occupied a room where business was transacted and a kitchen which provided the living quarters for the draper, his wife, baby and two brothers-in-law. A close ran hard by the shop and two blocks of houses which gave access to the upper dwellings; this was 'not infrequently some inches deep with water or mud, or the fluid part of every kind of filth, carelessly thrown down from unwillingness to go with it to the common receptacles'.[1] While Robbie was more fortunate than most, in that he was employed in a relatively safe and comfortable environment, protected from the elements, the hours frequently dragged by and boredom numbed his soul. But he rejoiced in the Sabbath. While others dreaded the deadly tedium of that day, reports from the mission field fuelled his fire for adventure.

Robbie was attentive, bright, eager to learn, and observant. He explored the wharves and quays of the burgeoning port of Glasgow, noting the construction of massive warehouses and new shipyards that built the first seagoing iron steamships which introduced the city and the Clyde to the world.

Robbie's increasing familiarity with the docks made him well-known among their denizens and he was particularly drawn to the East Indiamen, whose sailors readily 'swung the lamp' in response to Robbie's incessant speiring. His initial dream of travel was so enhanced by each visit that it encroached upon his waking hours, with such effect that he could retreat at will into his other world. By nineteen, Robert Burns had skimped and saved sufficient money for a ticket to the East.

Glasgow was in the van of the inexorable march of the Industrial Revolution, as it continued in nineteenth-century Britain, accompanied by the emergence of science and technology, the flourishing of literature and the arts, and the geographical exploration of lands beyond the seas. During this time, the Empire attained its apogee by force of arms and colonisation, promoting accretion of 'the blessings of civilisation' and ensuring that 'the light of the Gospel will shine in these benighted lands.'[2] Scots contributed handsomely in settling distant shores, but what of their birthplace? To many, outwith the country, it was an illusion contrived by Scott and rendered into stone by Victoria and Albert with the creation of Balmoral. Their Scotland was populated by a pious, impoverished people who endured the tyranny of the church and bowed to absentee landlords. In truth, it was 'an age of appalling social deprivation'.[3] The advent of the railways, which facilitated transport of coal and minerals from the Lanarkshire coalfields and elsewhere, was welcomed by shrewd industrialists who amassed great wealth from fresh enterprises. They founded breweries and distilleries, built brick, chemical, glass and ironworks, potteries, and factories for the manufacture of all kinds of machinery, especially locomotives. But in revolutionising shipbuilding, 'Clyde-built' was blazed abroad as the guarantee of excellence.

As Glasgow's industrial maw grew insatiably, it ingested workers from the length and breadth of Britain, many from rural backgrounds. By 1841, the population of Glasgow was over 274,000, of whom 16% were Irish-born. While there were traditional seasonal migrations, especially from Northern Ireland and the Highlands of Scotland, the decline of the cotton industry in Ulster, the 'rationalisation' of linen manufacture in that province, the plight of crofters in the north and north-west of Scotland and later 'the Great Hunger', witnessed migration on a massive scale in the 1840s.

In 1840–1841,[4] some of the 15,000 navvies who came to build the Edinburgh-Glasgow railway, descended on the village of Springburn, about a mile from the city centre and because of their nomadic existence and harsh working environment, they were regarded as amongst the least 'respectable' newcomers. The decline of the traditional rural economy in the Lowlands was now well-established.

In Glasgow, the flight of the middle classes from the city centre enhanced the malignant growth of the slum, a new phenomenon in Scots society. The burgeoning slum district had a population of over 20,000 around 1830, with the number rising annually as migrants poured into the city. House construction had not kept pace with the human flood and this was a factor in subsequent overcrowding. Slums were characterised by gross overpopulation, filth and disease and while they were found in every city in the United Kingdom, Glasgow was unique in the magnitude of its social problems. As the reports[5] of the Assistant Hand-Loom Weavers Commissioners observed:

> The wynds consist of long lanes, so narrow that a cart could with difficulty pass along them; out of these open the 'closes', which are courts about 15–20 feet square; round which the houses, mostly of three stories high, are built; the centre of the court is the dunghill, which is probably the most lucrative part of the estate to the laird in most instances, and which it would consequently be deemed an

invasion of the rights of the property to remove. The houses are for the most part let in flats, either to the lowest class of labourers or prostitutes, or to lodging keepers ... In the lower lodging houses, then, twelve and sometimes twenty persons of both sexes and all ages sleep promiscuously on the floor in varying degrees of nakedness. These places are, generally as regards dirt, damp and decay, such as no person of common humanity to animals would stable his horse in ... It is my firm belief that penury, diet, misery, drunkenness, disease and crime culminate in Glasgow to a pitch unparalleled in Great Britain.

Another contemporary observer, Dr Neil Arnott[6] noted that the central dunghill was 'of the most disgusting kind' and that the inhabitants of the labyrinth of wynds and closes 'actually hoarded their own dung in order to help pay the rent' and were 'worse off than wild animals which withdraw to a distance and conceal their ordure'.

In Glasgow, more than one-third of families lived in one room, lacking sanitation and clean water. The city's supply, of dubious quality, was drawn from communal wells, which in 1834 numbered thirty to water a population of over 200,000. Of these only fourteen were in good order. The rapid proliferation of industrial pollution and the gargantuan output of human excreta that overwhelmed the primitive sewerage system, were potent contributors to massive onslaughts of disease. The densely packed malnourished, without clean water or sanitation, lived in the miasmata of accumulated excrement; the perfect pabulum for bacterial and viral infections that flared against a backdrop of chronic disease.

Thousands died in the cholera epidemics of 1832, 1848 and 1853, while those who escaped fell in swathes to typhus in the outbreaks of 1837 and 1847. The vectors in the latter were lice that infested the rags, clothes and bedding of potential victims and whose spread was frequently aided by unscrupulous ship-owners and others who sold such items after the deaths of their owners. In the 'typhus-cholera quinquennium of 1845-49', Glasgow had a Crude Death Rate of forty per thousand; almost half a century before the discovery of bacteria, and almost a century before the discovery of effective treatments.

'Life in Scotland in the 1840s was competitive, unprotected, brutal and, for many, vile.[7] While epidemics of cholera and typhus scoured the wynds and closes of their human detritus, populations of grim tenements and ignominious slums were chronically depleted by tuberculosis, 'fever', gastrointestinal disease and respiratory infections. The overcrowded, inhabitants were defenceless victims. Such peals of children's laughter that echoed down the stairwells were frequently short-lived, stifled by the keening of grieving parents. Two decades later, there was little improvement: the mean age of males at death was 24.1 in town districts and for females, 27.4 years. Even in those days of rudimentary statistics, male children under the age of five accounted for 'the enormous proportion of 45.8 per cent' of male deaths in urban areas.[8]

What hope existed for this section of society as it strove to survive in an environment of black despair, charged with disease, crime and prostitution? The few who could, saved and quit this hell forever.

Chapter II

James Brooke

A few years before Robbie's birth, a young lieutenant in the 18th Native Infantry, one of the many regiments in the Honourable East India Company's Bengal Army, was gazetted Sub-Assistant Commissary-General, a post for which he was 'totally unfitted'. The appointment afforded abundant leisure for the destruction of the local fauna, in the best tradition of the English gentleman; but unusually, this young officer began to read widely and voraciously. In contrast to Burns, this man, James Brooke, was a privileged scion of the English middle class. Born in the European enclave of Secrore in the holy city of Benares, on 29 April 1803, James was the second son of Thomas Brooke, chief of the East India Company's provincial court at Moorshedabad.[1] He remained in India until the age of twelve when he was returned to the guardianship of his paternal grandmother at Reigate and Charles Kegan, a retired Indian civil servant who lived in Bath. Spenser St John, Brooke's Private Secretary and subsequent biographer, wrote that James 'had been indulged and petted by all around him, as he had a lovable disposition.'[2] The contemporary New Zealand historian, Nicholas Tarling, added that 'no doubt the circumstances in which he lived brought out the character of a rather spoiled child that St John discreetly depicts.'[3]

Young James's feelings upon enrolment at Norwich Grammar School can be imagined. Alone, he faced the rigours of an English education after the comfort and subservience of an Anglo-Indian home, the indulgence of a doting grandmother and the gentility of the Kegan ménage. He disliked 'gerund-grinding' but he shared his school-fellows' affection for their drawing master John Crome, 'Old Crome' the landscape painter, who often painted small cottage scenes during class, with his pupils crowded round him.[4] James also learned to sail on the river Wensum where he saved a fellow pupil by diving to retrieve him from under an upturned boat. He remained at school for about two or three years before absconding. Downcast at the start of a new term, he returned to find that his great friend, George Western, had gone to sea as a midshipman, so James promptly borrowed a guinea and took the stagecoach to Surrey and

Grandmother Brooke. Afraid to enter the house, he skulked in the grounds until discovered by servants. Kegan, when informed, journeyed to Surrey and escorted the boy to Norwich, but the school would not readmit him and he returned to Bath. James then resisted daily tuition and frustrated all attempts at formal education, despite his parents' return home to retirement near Bath and a brief stay at another school.

At fifteen, Brooke set off for India as a cadet, being commissioned as an Ensign on 11 May 1819 in the 6th Native Infantry. He was promoted to Lieutenant on 21 November 1821.

In 1823, Lord Amherst became Governor-General of Bengal and soon afterwards the King of Burma demanded cession of the whole of the eastern half of the province. The Burmese then drove out the British garrison stationed on the island of Shapporree at the mouth of the river Naef and an army was sent to capture Bengal. After the expected rout of the British, Amherst was to be bound in golden fetters and led into the King's presence. Such 'presumptuous conduct made the continuance of peace impossible' and Amherst declared war on 24 February 1824.[5]

Brooke was ordered to join the invading army on its overland march through Assam, and while still underemployed, he chanced to hear the commanding general complain that he had no light cavalry to act as scouts. Brooke immediately offered to raise a volunteer troop from those infantrymen who could ride, provided that 'He might have his own way.' His irregulars were effective and Brooke was mentioned in despatches for his part in a skirmish near Rungpore on 27 January 1825.[1] Two days later, he was shot in the chest and left for dead until removed to safety, to survive the immediate effects of what must have been a near-fatal wound, long before the advent of aseptic surgery and antibacterial drugs. A prolonged and stormy convalescence extended into five years' leave in England.

The nature of Brooke's injury has been a topic of conjecture among his biographers and other writers. Owen Rutter, a noted author who spent five years in the British North Borneo Civil Service, recounted a story, learned from the son of an intimate friend of Brooke, that James had been struck in the pelvis by a musket shot.[6] This anecdote was the basis of his alleged impotence, a broken engagement nine years later and his life-long bachelorhood. Sylvia, the wife of the third Raja Brooke, subscribed to the theory,[7] but there is no mention of the nature of the wound in James Brooke's military record or elsewhere. It is significant that Brooke acknowledged the existence of an illegitimate son many years after the child's birth in 1834.

At the end of long leave, Brooke set out for India with ample time to meet the Honourable Company's deadline, but his ship, the East Indiaman, *Carn Brea Castle*, was driven aground by a freak summer storm on Brook Ledge, near Mottiston on the Isle of Wight.[8] The following morning, the swell prevented rescue by local fishing boats, but the Coastguard, Lieutenant Dornford, mustered a crew and their cutter succeeded in taking off the passengers, East India Company employees and their families. Brooke lost his new-gained health and his kit. The Company granted him a further six months' furlough, provided that he reported for duty in Calcutta by 30 July 1830, but inclement weather again frustrated Brooke's return. The *Castle Huntly*, an East Indiaman of 1311 tons, eventually berthed in Madras on 18 July, too late for the lieutenant to reach Bengal by land. After an unsuccessful attempt to secure temporary employment with the Company, Brooke resigned and requested that he might be allowed to return to England in the same ship. The Madras Government complied and the Company's Court directed that his name be struck off the Army List from 13 December 1827, 'in consequence of his absence from India exceeding five years.'[1]

When Brooke left the army, St John stated that the decision was for the best, as Brooke was really unsuited for any post that demanded steady application. Brooke stayed on board the *Castle Huntly* which was to return to England by way of the Indian Archipelago and China. She left Madras for Penang, which Brooke found enchanting, then on to Singapore where he observed the Chinese whom he was already determined to dislike.

In the preface to his life of Brooke, St John wrote that his subject was 'one of the noblest and best of men',[9] but in common with many biographies penned in Victorian times, there is scarcely a hint of blemish. Can one really accept that James Brooke, the wilful schoolboy, is transfigured into a stainless soldier statesman on reaching maturity? However, even St John alludes to misconduct, but before Brooke set foot in Borneo. While aboard the *Castle Huntly*, Brooke committed 'enough imprudences' at known ports of call 'to have cut off his career forever'.

Gertrude Jacob, another Victorian biographer, recounted an adventure in Canton where Brooke and some other men allegedly disguised themselves as Chinese and slipped through a gateway to the town during the Feast of Lanterns.[10] Once inside the forbidden grounds, they threw off their disguises, broke some precious lanterns and barely escaped with their lives. Brooke eventually returned to England to ponder his future and to thole a broken engagement.

A projected trading venture to China ended in a considerable financial loss, then Brooke's father died in 1835, leaving him £30,000 with which he bought and fitted out the *Royalist*, a schooner of 142 tons. After a shakedown cruise to the Mediterranean with a hand-picked crew, the *Royalist* finally stood out to sea from Devonport on 16 December 1838, for Rio de Janeiro. The passage took almost two months and during a refit, Brooke[11] noted that while the slave trade was prohibited by the Brazilian government, the law was lax. 'The trade is therefore as briskly carried on as ever just outside the harbour of Rio ... Surely more effective measures might be enforced if the Christian nations of Europe were resolved to unite in the effort.'

Two weeks later, *Royalist* sailed for the Cape of Good Hope and on the 15 March 1839, beat into Table Bay in the teeth of a 'fiery south-easter'. Brooke hastily effected repairs and put to sea on 29 March, passing through the Straits of Sunda and Banca before anchoring in Singapore harbour in the last week of May. Brooke was immediately impressed by the town, 'the aspect of the place is at once neat and highly pleasing', but he expressed disappointment at the lack of cultivation in the interior of the island.

Chapter III

Brooke, Raja of Sarawak

Before he left England, Brooke[1] wrote that 'On the commencement of the healthy season, I purpose sailing from Singapore, and proceeding without loss of time to Malludu Bay,' a British possession at the north-eastern extremity of Borneo. But according to Rutter[2], who heard the story from the widow of the second Raja Brooke, James changed his plans after meeting Mr Bonham, the Governor of Singapore. Bonham was riding one morning, shortly before the arrival of the *Royalist*, when he reined in his horse to watch a Chinese boat unloading ballast. The animal reared, kicked a pile of stones which had been flung ashore and Bonham glimpsed an object sparkling in the rubble; this proved to be a stone split by his horse's hooves. Further inquiry revealed that the rock contained antimony and that the boat hailed from the Sarawak river.

Bonham was a kind and hospitable host and the pair sailed round the island. Brooke was saddened to find that:

> The site of the ancient city of Johore is now scarcely discernible ...
> Is it not sad to think that kingdoms are laid low, and the inhabitants
> oppressed and dispersed, whenever they come within the grasp of
> European civilisation? How painful the reflection, that, wherever the
> white man has set his foot-mark, there the print of the native foot is
> obliterated, and that as the tender plant withers beneath his tread, so
> wither the aboriginal inhabitant of the soil![3]

On learning of Brooke's itinerary, Bonham told him of his find and suggested that Sarawak offered better prospects, not only for its minerals, than Maludu Bay. The Malay Governor had recently succoured a shipwrecked British crew and Bonham promised Brooke a letter of introduction, if he would convey a gift from the Singapore Chamber of Commerce, in recognition of the kindness shown to the survivors. Brooke was also informed that:

> ... the sultan of Borneo Proper [Brunei] is favourably inclined to the
> English, and hates the Dutch.

From Borneo Proper, Brooke hoped:

> ... to penetrate the interior ... From the capital and with the kingly protection, much may be done.[4]

Two weeks later, he had decided to sail to Brunei:

> On my way to the capital, I propose looking at the coast as minutely as circumstances will allow, and visiting Sarawak – the place whence small vessels bring the ore of antimony.[5]

The *Royalist* left Singapore on 27 July 1839 and was off the coast of Borneo on 1 August. A fortnight later, after surveying a stretch of coast, Brooke dispatched his gig up the Sarawak River to communicate with the authorities. The boat returned next day accompanied by a large perahu sent by the Raja to welcome him. *Royalist* proceeded cautiously upstream to what is now Kuching, where he was received by the Raja Muda Hassim who ruled the territory on behalf of his uncle, the Sultan of Brunei. At that time, the Raja Muda was beset by rebellion which he dismissed as inconsequential, but Brooke gleaned that it was more serious than the Raja gave out; it was also hinted that Brooke should remain to intimidate the rebels. Hassim initially struck Brooke as 'a man of *first rate ability*, and very partial to the English'[6] and he granted Brooke permission to travel to some of the Malay towns, but cautioned against going upriver or to any of the Dyak settlements that were not well-disposed to his government. During his stay, Brooke inferred:

> That the political ascendancy of the English is paramount and that they might, if they pleased, by means of an offensive and defensive alliance between the two powers [Britain and Brunei], gain the entire trade of the north-west coast of Borneo ...[7]

Brooke then decided to support the Raja Muda and with the *Royalist* he helped put down the insurrection before returning to Singapore and on to Celebes.

Royalist was away for a year before refitting in Singapore where Brooke resolved to return to Borneo. In late August, he learned that the rebels had been defeated but he was still in Sarawak in early October. The

Raja Muda begged him not to leave and when Brooke intimated that he planned to do so, Hassim offered him the territory of Siniawan and Sarawak, its government and its trade, if he would remain.

> I could at once have obtained this grant, but I preferred interposing a delay[8] ... The only inquiry was, whether the Rajah had the right and authority to make over the country to me, and this I was assured he had.[9]

Brooke declined all treaties until the conflict was over and he threw in his lot with Hassim. Papers were signed that made him Resident of Sarawak and the country, government and trade were transferred to him, to be held under the Sultan of Brunei, with all its revenues and dependencies, on payment of two thousand Spanish dollars for the first year and one thousand annually thereafter. Brooke agreed:

> ... to buy a vessel, and bring down trade to the place, in return for which I was assured of antimony-ore in plenty ... [10]

Brooke's appointment was subsequently confirmed by the Sultan of Brunei and in 1841 he became the first white Raja of Sarawak, founding a dynasty that lasted until 1946 with cession to the British crown.

Between 1841 and 1847, Brooke busied himself with government and attempts to bring peace to the coast. In considering his initial plan for Sarawak, he decided that he would retain the antimony monopoly and thereby gather a net annual revenue of £1,800–£2,000.[11] The Chinese would work the gold and trade from the coast would develop. Brooke was also determined to crush piracy and in 1843 he met Captain Keppel, the senior naval officer in the Straits Settlements. Keppel was on board his corvette at Penang and he immediately made a 'voluntary and most generous offer of bringing the *Dido* to the coast of Borneo for the extirpation of Piracy'.[12] Brooke and Keppel agreed that the only way of ridding the coast of this menace was to destroy the pirates' lairs in the interior of the country. They embarked for Borneo on 1 May and began their assault on the Saribas later that month, continuing with strikes along the Batang Lupar, plundering and burning, leaving Keppel to conclude that 'The punishment we had inflicted was severe.'[13] *Dido* carried eighteen 32-pounders, a detachment of marines and was accompanied by the Honourable Company's steamer, *Phlegethon*. Keppel was then recalled to China, to be succeeded by Sir Edward Belcher in HMS *Samarang*. Also at this time,

Brooke appointed Henry Wise as his agent.

In 1845, Admiral Cochrane appeared off Brunei with a squadron of seven ships, demanding reparation for the capture and enslavement of two British subjects, lascars, who had been members of the crew of the merchantman, *Sultana*. Cochrane fought a battle off Maludu on 19 August before attacking and seizing Brunei the following year.

Robbie read of this and Brooke's exploits in Sarawak when the news eventually filtered to the British press. He also noticed the flood of raw materials such as cotton, exotic timbers, sugar and tobacco that inundated the expanding port, driving manufacture and laying the foundations of industrial empires. But above the clamour, Robbie heard the vociferous demands of Glasgow's merchants and Chamber of Commerce as they sought fresh trading opportunities to sustain the wealth of the city. He resolved to seek his fortune in Borneo.

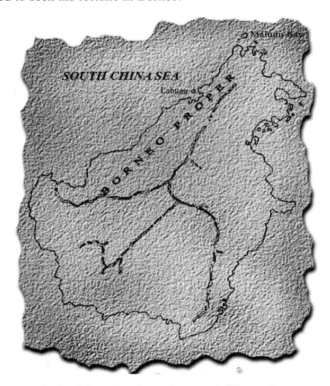

In the 19th century, Sarawak was part of Borneo Proper.

Political map of modern Borneo showing the disposition of the Malaysian states of Sarawak and Sabah and the independent country of Brunei. Kalimantan is part of Indonesia.

Chapter IV

Borneo

W hen Robbie dreamt by the fire at home in Glasgow, the Island of Borneo was indiscernible, concealed by rolling black clouds and torrential rain, the like of which he had never seen.

The third largest island on earth straddles the equator between 7° north and 4° south, some three hundred miles east of the Malaysian Peninsula at its nearest point. This four-sided mass is larger than the whole of France and its name was probably introduced by the Portuguese as a corruption of Burni, now Brunei. But the island was known long before the Portuguese, Spanish, Dutch and British made landfall. Evidence of a pre-neolithic culture has been found in coastal regions and the northern shore afforded important ports of call in the 9th century AD. Indeed, according to Chinese records, there were embassies at the Imperial Court between 600 and 1500 AD and it is generally accepted that they originated in settlements on Borneo's west coast.[1] The territory is now divided politically between the sovereign states of Brunei Darussalam, Indonesia and Malaysia. Its northern shore, which witnessed chicanery, mass-murder and piracy in the nineteenth century, was also the theatre of contention between Burns and Brooke.

Geologically, Borneo consists mainly of young sedimentary rocks that include limestones with fabulous cave formations, once home to early man, now refuge to millions of swiftlets whose nests are pillaged for soup. There are no active volcanoes but some old volcanic deposits are found in south-east Sabah. Borneo, with Sumatra, Java and a multitude of smaller islands, formed part of the mainland of South-East Asia until geologically recent times. Geographically, Sabah and Sarawak to a lesser extent, have a flat coastal plain that rises to rugged uplands towards the interior. In Sarawak, the mountains, which lie close to the sea in the south-west, form part of the frontier with the Indonesian state of Kalimantan, as they run towards Sabah in the north-east.

The greater part of the now small country of Brunei is low coastal plain in contrast to Sabah, where the Crocker Range, which averages from 457–914 metres in height, peaks as an isolated horst in Mount (Gunung)

Kinabalu at 4095.2 metres. Gunung Kinabalu, the Chinese Widow, is one of the highest mountains between the Himalayas and New Guinea, rising 'sheer and wonderful above a thousand hills'.[2]

The climate is tropical. Coastal temperatures climb from a minimum of around 21°C to about 32°C and humidity is high. Although the rainfall varies, most areas receive between 200 and 400 cm each year. Two monsoons govern the climate, the north-east prevails between late October and February, deluging south-west Sarawak and the east coast of Sabah, whereas the south-west blows from April to August, carrying most rain to the west coast of Sabah.

Borneo's river systems are extensive and gave the indigenous peoples and early explorers access to the interior, unless the way was barred by insurmountable rapids. The rivers also appear to have been important in determining the distribution of some mammals by forming boundaries to migration. The Rejang is the principal river of Sarawak and the Kinabatagnan (the Chinese River) ranks first in Sabah. Both featured prominently in Burns's expeditions but he died without having seen the latter. The former drains one-third of the entire state and although it is less than one-tenth the length of the Amazon, it has one of the highest outputs of any river in the world. The Rejang in flood is awesome and it elicits more than a frisson of fear. Its waters rise and fall with extraordinary rapidity, five metres in thirty-six hours in the writer's experience. In the past, the torrent restricted raiding-parties foraging for human heads from upstream longhouses, but today, the river carries considerable traffic from the sea to the head of navigation. 'Ekspres' passenger services transport Chinese traders, Orang Ulu ('Upriver People'), a few European tourists and provisions from Sibu to Kapit and beyond. Small tankers carry fuel for longhouse generators, and pugnacious tugboats punch courses between rocks and shoals, towing rafts of huge logs. Not all the timber is secure, loose trunks and trees hurtle seawards threatening navigation, while local longboats, powered by outboard motors, criss-cross the currents in search of safe water. All sounds are subordinate to the roar of the Rejang in flood.

Evergreens of various species form the bulk of the island's vegetation. Tall lowland and hill forests are dominated by dipterous trees of which two hundred and eighty-seven types live in Borneo. The Pelagus forest, traversed by Burns, is a fine example of the lowland variety, where trees thrive in poor clay soil in symbiotic relationships with fungi. The canopy is formed by dipterocarps 45 or more metres in height and shade-dwelling trees between 24 and 36 metres; while shrubs, palms and aroids constitute the sparse ground cover. The dipterocarps include most of the commercially valuable timber, but many other species abound, along with lianes, small flowering plants and ferns that grow as epiphytes on the larger trees.

Much of the Bornean coastline is fringed by nipah palm and mangrove swamps, where the turbid, brackish waters of the estuaries and meandering tributaries support myriads of insects, crustaceae, fish, birdlife in profusion and Crocodylus porosus, the man-eating, estuarine or saltwater crocodile. Some of the world's most exotic creatures and plants inhabit the forests, among them the orang utan, the rare clouded leopard, rhinoceros, tapir, fish that climb trees, flying lizards and snakes, birds with massive hornbills, carnivorous plants and Rafflesia, a stemless, leafless parasite whose flowers may reach more than one metre in diameter.

The indigenous peoples of Sabah and Sarawak belong to the Austronesian group, considered to have been the earliest inhabitants who migrated from Asia and who first colonised the coasts and river mouths.[3] They introduced stone tools and agricultural practices and when other settlers arrived, they withdrew into the interior. The subsequent distribution of this population is difficult to resolve; in the case of the Iban, for example, their migrations were not methodical. Resolution is further complicated by deficiencies in current demographic procedures; for instance, census classifications make no allowance for native tongue. However, in Sarawak, which now includes the territory explored by Burns and acquired by the Brookes, it is possible to assign the population into three groups: first, the coastal people, namely the Malays and Melanau; next the Lowland group that consists of the Iban and Bedayuh and last, the Orang Ulu. The 'Upriver People' include the Kayan, Kenyah and remaining indigenous cultures.

Such names were apparently applied by the coastal inhabitants in the main. But before the advent of the Brookes and to a lesser extent today, those native to Sabah and Sarawak, identified with their abode or, more often, with a river in that locality. This practice, which is analogous to the Scots, 'of that ilk', originated before British rule, when the river basins were administered by Pangerans on behalf of the Sultan of Brunei.

The enchorial peoples of Sarawak are often described as 'Dyaks' but this is a misnomer. In 1896, Roth[4] stated that 'The term Dyak appears to have been given a more widespread significance than it is entitled to, and people are thereby misled.' More recently, Omar,[5] wrote that the identification of groups by externally imposed names 'more often than not generates a confusion in identity and belonging among the people concerned.' Like the second Raja Brooke, she maintained that the word 'Dyak' and its cognates occur in many Sarawakian languages and simply mean 'upriver'. The British evidently repeated the Dutch error of describing all inland or upriver peoples as Dyaks.

Burns and Brooke had special relationships with the Kayan and Iban, respectively. Both peoples are believed to have originated in Kalimantan (formerly Dutch Borneo) and to have migrated into Sarawak up to two to three hundred years ago. In Burns's day, the Kayan mainly occupied the region of the Baram river and its principal tributaries and were greatly feared by their neighbours. Like the Iban, they lived in longhouses which even today stretch for a hundred metres or more along the terraced bank of a river or some other favoured site. Again, like the Iban, they hunted with sumpitan (blowpipe) and spear, but in war, according to Burns, they favoured the sword.

Victorians who knew of Borneo, often described it as an island paradise. The distinguished observer and sometime Secretary to the Government of Labuan, Hugh Low,[6] wrote that:

> The climate of Borneo, like that of most of the Eastern islands, has been found exceedingly healthy to persons whose avocations do not render great exposure necessary.

However, this was penned in 1848 and reflects the almost total ignorance of infectious diseases at that time. Bacterial, parasitic and viral infections were, as now, endemic. Malaria was omnipresent, sporadic epidemics, especially of cholera, diphtheria, typhoid and smallpox decimated the population and few withstood these onslaughts. Visits to old Christian burial grounds today, evoke sad images of maternal and childhood deaths in small expatriate communities, while the morbidity and mortality among the local populace can only be surmised. Burns, like Brooke, was frequently wracked by 'fever' and Brooke almost succumbed to that and to smallpox.

Today's visitors to Kuching, the capital of Sarawak, mostly arrive by air and their first glimpse of northern Borneo is usually the vast brown stain of the Sarawak river draining into the turquoise South China Sea. A narrow coastal strip of white sand delineates a dark green carpet of jungle, pierced by serpentine rivers the colour of molten chocolate, and mountains on the horizon reach above the clouds. A century and a half ago, Europeans knew little of the place. The region was inimical to foreigners and dangerous shoals and sunken reefs created hazards for the most competent navigator, save one, Captain the Honourable Henry Keppel, RN. Redoubtable and intrepid, he 'actually sailed by the best Admiralty chart eighty miles inland, and over the tops of mountains!'[7] The sea held other dangers. Pirates destroyed trade and ravaged the coast on and offshore, while others hunted human heads. This was the country of Burns and Brooke, whose lives are part of the warp and weft of Borneo's kaleidoscopic historical tapestry.

SACRED
TO THE MEMORIES OF
ISABELLA CAROLINE VELGE
WHO DEPARTED THIS LIFE ON THE 28TH NOVEMBER 1853
BORN 22ND FEBRUARY THE SAME YEAR. AGED 9 MONTHS & 6
DAYS
ROBERT MALCOLM EVANS
WHO DEPARTED THIS LIFE ON THE 16TH JANUARY 1856
BORN 28TH OCTOBER 1855, AGED 2 MONTHS & 19 DAYS
ANNA MARIA EVANS
WHO DEPARTED THIS LIFE ON THE 24TH JANUARY 1856
BORN 17TH JULY 1831, AGED 24 YEARS 6 MONTHS 7 17 DAYS
EDWARD NAGEL EVANS
WHO DEPARTED THIS LIFE ON THE 24TH JANUARY 1856
BORN 12TH AUGUST 1852, AGED 3 YEARS 5 MONTHS & 12 DAYS
LOUISA AUGUSTA EVANS
WHO DEPARTED THIS LIFE ON THE 2ND FEBRUARY 1856
BORN 15TH APRIL 1851, AGED 4 YEARS 9 MONTHS & 17 DAYS
FREDERICK THEODORE VELGE
WHO DEPARTED THIS LIFE ON THE 8TH FEBRUARY 1856
BORN 1ST OCTOBER 1855, AGED 1 YEAR 4 MONTHS & 8 DAYS

THIS TABLET IS ERECTED AS A LAST TESTIMONY OF THE
LOVE AND AFFECTION OF THEIR FATHER AND
GRANDFATHER
J H VELCH

The Evans and Velge family memorial, Malacca, Malaysia. A grim reminder of the devastation caused by infectious diseases before the advent of immunisation and antibiotics. The cause of death of those who died in 1856 was diphtheria.

Chapter V

Sir James Brooke

In 1846, Brooke's agent, Henry Wise, called upon a Mr James Augustus St John in London to express thanks for the tone of articles that St John, an author, had written about Borneo in the *Morning Chronicle* and in various periodicals. St John's third son, Spenser, was exhorted by Wise to seek an appointment with Brooke. But St John senior often said that Wise was too enthusiastic and about a year later, he told his son that 'Our friend [Wise] has been letting out a great many things about Mr Brooke: he accuses him of all sorts of crimes but says these must be kept a profound secret. Perhaps you had better give up the idea of going to Borneo'.[1]

Brooke, accompanied by Hugh Low, sailed for England in 1847, leaving Sarawak in the care of his cousin, Arthur Crookshank. After an enforced stopover in Ceylon, they reached Southampton on 1 October where they were met by family and friends, including Captain Keppel. Henry Wise was the first to entertain Brooke at a large dinner at his home where he made 'a most fulsome speech' praising Brooke. When Spenser St John was told of this by his father, he immediately 'set Wise down as a humbug'.[2] He later discovered that Wise's enmity towards Brooke stemmed from the time when Wise could not induce Brooke to entrust him with full powers to form a great company. This enterprise was to acquire Sarawak for a very large sum, of which Wise would keep half.

On 19 January 1848, the *Straits Times* reported:

We hear that H. E. Mr Brooke, Governor of the (intended) Settlement of Labuan will be knighted by Majesty; after which ceremony he will quit Europe and may be expected to arrive here by the March steamer. Deputy governor Napier and Mr Colonial Secretary Low will, it is said, arrive here by the same opportunity.

From the English journals, extracts from which are given elsewhere, it will be seen that Mr Brooke has been entertained by the Queen and nobility of England, lionized by the citizens of London, idolized by the Church Mission folk and ridiculed by *Punch* and, some of his contemporaries – what more, and what next!

Brooke was indeed feted. He was given the freedom of the City of London and membership of its Corporation as a Fishmonger and Goldsmith, in addition to honorary membership of the principal clubs. Dinner followed dinner. The *Illustrated London News* reported that Brooke was present at a 'grand entertainment at the Mansion House' in honour of HRH the Duke of Cambridge, where the Lord Mayor proposed the health of Her Majesty's Commissioner for Borneo, extolling 'The extraordinary exertions of that distinguished man in distant and uncivilised countries'. The toast was drunk with 'great enthusiasm' and in reply, Brooke declared that 'the reception which he had met with today fully repaid him for the exertions which he had made and which he trusted would be attended with good results which the company honoured him by anticipating.' A short time later, Brooke was invited to a Grand Ball given by the Lady Mayoress and the following week he appeared at the chief table at the Lord Mayor's Banquet as Rajah of Sarawak.

Oxford conferred the honorary degree of Doctor of Civil Law on 25 November[3] and he was dined by the great and noble, besides being a frequent guest at their country seats. Not only did the Ministers of the Crown show their appreciation of Brooke's achievements, he was received by Her Majesty at Windsor. This show was in sharp contrast to the initial disgraceful treatment of the explorer, H. M. Stanley, when he returned to England from Africa in 1872.

At Windsor, Prince Albert's German valet de chambre advised Brooke 'very discreetly' that 'a black or blue coat, white waistcoat, white cravat, tight pantaloons, with black stockings was the right thing, – your shoes without buckles, and neither hat nor gloves'. Thus attired, Raja Brooke was presented to the Queen who spoke with him for nearly ten minutes after dinner. He then endured Albert before being presented to Lady Peel 'et hoc genus omne' which he translated as 'all them there nobs' in a letter to a niece.[4]

Brooke was busy in London. He attended a public meeting to send a Christian mission to Borneo and a Mr McDougall was appointed to the charge. McDougall was to become the first Anglican Bishop of Sarawak and a bitter enemy of Brooke's biographer, Spenser St John. Sir Francis Grant, President of the Royal Academy, painted Brooke's portrait and Brooke was appointed Governor of Labuan and Consul-General of Sarawak. Spenser St John did not heed his father's advice and became

Brooke's Secretary.

On 1 November 1847, Captain Keppel was given command of HMS *Maeander*, a new square-rigged frigate of forty-four guns and on 31 December, he wrote in his diary that:

> The next three or four years are likely to be the most eventful of my life.[5]

Then, in a postscript to 1847, Keppel added:

> I cannot close my diary this year without mention of the sore trouble in which my friend Brooke was involved. The commencement, indeed, of the persecution from which he emerged stainless, but at the cost of mental anxiety which ultimately caused his death.

He then summarised Brooke's dealings with Wise from his viewpoint. The size of Brooke's entourage caused them to take passage in *Maeander* via the Cape. St John later wrote that this was:

> ... a most unwise determination, as during this long voyage were sown the seeds of strife and heartburning, which sprouted and grew, and later on ripened into very unpleasant fruit.[6]

Brooke's company included Hugh Low, Secretary to the Government of Labuan; Mr Napier, the prospective Lieutenant-Governor of the island and his family; St John, Brooke's newly appointed Secretary, and Scott the surveying engineer at Labuan. St John was to write, 'There is no greater error in the world than turning vessels of war into passenger-ships, particularly when ladies are concerned. Every spot is occupied beforehand.'[7] Keppel was also inconvenienced. The guns on *Maeander's* main deck were dismounted as far for'ard as the main-mast, the gun ports were made into windows and the deck was divided into cabins, giving the ship the appearance of an Indiaman, without the accommodation. Keppel's cabin was called the 'saloon', his servants 'waiters', 'and when the ship gave an extra plunge, sundry 'brandies and sodas' were called for.'[8]

Maeander weighed anchor from Spithead on 1 February 1848 and was struck by a head sea and heavy winds as soon as she left harbour. The luggage 'was banged about, all was discomfort'. *Maeander* made for Plymouth before weighing from the Sound two days later. The weather worsened and Keppel was forced to run for Cork and shelter. Five days later they were off to Madeira and they reached Funchal on 23 February. Such relief! Brooke and his party attended balls, parties and picnics before embarking for Rio with heavy hearts. King Neptune boarded the ship on 10 March when *Maeander* crossed the Line, then it was off to Rio for four days before Captain Keppel gave his passengers a course in advanced seamanship.

On 27 March, Keppel 'Determined, with my cargo, on not calling at Simon's Bay. Provisioned accordingly.'[9] *Maeander* was under weigh at daybreak the following morning and ran south with the land breeze. Nine days later the weather turned 'dirty' and water had to be baled out of the fore-cabin. On 19 April *Maeander* reached Prince Edward's Island in 46° 23′ S and Keppel added, 'Not often made by ships going to India. Best and shortest route though!'

On 20 April, he noted that *Maeander* had logged twelve knots for eight successive hours. Keppel was 'great-circle sailing' and while he did not go sufficiently far south, it was 'quite far enough' for St John, with 'heavy winds, rough seas, and bitter cold'. Keppel was an enthusiast, known by 'friend and enemy' as the red-haired devil, he 'had a passion for making rapid passages, and carried on sail until the ship was half buried in the sea: the consequences were loss of spars and canvas to the ship, and loss of comfort for all'.[10] The ship's company and passengers grumbled in vain.

Maeander was once more within the limits of the East Indian Station on 26 April and one week later she encountered heavy squalls which damaged the bowsprit. Miss Napier celebrated her nineteenth birthday on 5 May with champagne and a dance in the fore-cabin. 'Think there is something in the wind between her and Low!' wrote Keppel in his diary; the couple were married in St Andrew's Church, Singapore on 12 August by *Maeander*'s chaplain.

The weather improved as *Maeander* pointed nor'east and she was off Christmas Island at 3 a.m. on 12 May; eight days later she dropped anchor in Singapore to everyone's relief. Brooke made very few references to the voyage in his correspondence except to note that *Maeander* was an unhappy ship. St John remarked:

I am afraid that the passengers, not excepting Mr Brooke himself, were the original cause of the troubles on board.[11]

Brooke arrived in Singapore on 20 May 1848, where he was met by a guard of honour of fifty sepoys and fifty police peons. All the military officers in the Settlement were on parade, resplendent in full dress. *Maeander* fired a seventeen-gun salute when Brooke disembarked and this was echoed by the garrison's batteries as Her Majesty's First Governor of Labuan came ashore. He was subsequently informed that he had been appointed Knight Commander of the Bath. Rutter and others stated that 'this recognition left him unmoved ... he found his K.C.B. an empty honour.'

But Brooke was ambivalent. Nine years earlier he had written to Templer,

> One thing I regret not having tried to effect whilst at home, and that is getting a knighthood, a civic knighthood. You know me well enough to believe that such a distinction would never be sought by me except to answer some purpose.
>
> I believe the mere name would be very useful to me with natives and Europeans in this country – at home, I would not accept it, or wear the title, and though convinced of its utility, I will not beg or ask it; there are beggars enough in England. If they please to give it me on public grounds, as a barren reward, to facilitate a praiseworthy object, I would accept it.[12]

The topic reappeared three years later when Brooke wrote to his mother:

> You must think me very silly to ask to be made a knight! it is not that I care about knighthood, or that I would seek it in England; but any honour conferred upon me in my present position, is an indirect recognition of this place, and honours here, and in England, are very different. Here, that is at Singapore, as a knight, I should have no equal; and amongst the natives it would be important indeed, for it would proclaim me a chief, greater than the governor of Singapore, or any other on this side Calcutta ... – and remember now, I shall be a Tory knight ...[13]

After an absence from England of three months and five days, passengers and crew were avid for news. Keppel was stunned by the revolution in France, a new republic had been declared and Louis Philippe was in exile in England. Keppel also learned of the death of the former Commander-in-Chief, Admiral Inglefield, in Bombay, 'from wearing cocked hat in the sun' but the official cause was dysentery contracted in Madras.

Brooke's investiture took place on 22 August in the Public Assembly Rooms, Singapore. At one end of the room a dais had been constructed across its entire width and two steps above this was a chair representing a throne, under a canopy of crimson velvet edged with gold lace.

> The whole apartment was very tastefully decorated with flags, which produced an agreeable effect while the main entrance of the building outside was ornamented with a variety of green branches, shrubs and flowers.[14]

Two hundred and forty spectators in 'comfortable seats' watched the procession advance on red cloth to the throne, while at the other end of the room, *Maeander's* detachment of Marines faced the throne as a guard of honour for the Representative of the Crown, Lt Governor Napier. The ship's band played in the gallery.

However, the editor of a local newspaper was not invited. This accidental or deliberate oversight led to a succession of amusing articles supposedly belittling to the colony. Some of these were reprinted in the British press and were even mentioned in the House of Commons. St John observed that it was a pity that the investiture had not taken place in Sarawak.

Chapter VI

Burns and Old Singapore

R obbie's dream became reality when he boarded a ship bound for Singapore by way of Batavia, the capital of the former Dutch East Indies. The *Princess Royal*,[1] a square-sterned barque of 249 tons registered in Liverpool, was worked by a crew of eleven under the command of a seasoned Master, Captain Robert Sinclair.

Robbie occupied the only passenger berth at a probable cost of about twelve pounds. There is no record of the transaction, which was most likely negotiated between passenger and skipper. The price of a ticket seems ridiculous today but it is a reasonable estimate. In 1854, the cost of cabin accommodation from Liverpool to Melbourne aboard the *Donald McKay*,[2] a vessel of 3,500 tons, was seventeen pounds, which included food in specified quantities from provisions listed on the ticket. Mess utensils and bedding were provided by the passenger. Nine years later, a similar passage in steerage aboard the *Great Victoria*,[3] of 3,500 tons, cost twenty-six pounds five shillings.

The barque entered the port of Glasgow on 7 May 1846[1] and lay at berth four on the south side of the harbour from where she made brief visits to Greenock and Liverpool, before proceeding to the Broomielaw. Then, on 16 June, she cast off with a mixed cargo that included 550,015 yards of plain cotton, 12,000 pounds weight of cotton yarn, paint, and a piano. After calling briefly at Greenock, the *Princess Royal* cleared for sea the following day and set course for the Dutch East Indies.

Robbie reached Singapore on 27 October,[4] and after being advertised 'for freight or charter' in the local press, the *Princess Royal* sailed for Bombay on 13 November. In those days, losses at sea in storms, by fire and through acts of piracy were common and on 24 February 1849, the barque struck Lonsdale Reef, Port Phillip Heads, Australia.[5] Captain Sinclair was unaware that the light on Shortland's Bluff had been moved and after ordering the first mate to stand off until daylight, went below.

The *Princess Royal* hit the rocks at 3.00 a.m., broke in two on the third bump and quickly sank in a heavy south-west gale, leaving only the mizen cross-pieces above water. The rapid appraisal of the ship's plight by

Pilot Macpherson enabled the crew to abandon her without loss of life, although the cargo of rice, sugar and tea was forfeit to the elements.

When Robbie disembarked in Singapore, the port had existed for twenty-seven years, since Thomas Stamford Raffles successfully negotiated the foundation of a 'factory' or trading post in exchange for British protection and an annual payment to the local Malay Temenggong or chief. The new Malay ruler adopted the style 'Sultan of Johore' and took up residence about a mile north of the Singapore river. The royal compound formed the nucleus of the small Malay community and when news of the establishment of the free port of Singapore spread, immigrants flocked from places outwith the Malay peninsula to this new, safer and more profitable trading centre.

The town grew rapidly and by July 1845, the population was 57,421, of whom 336 were European – 204 men and 132 women.[6] As Singapore prospered, it was divided into two parts known colloquially as Twa Po (Big Town) at the mouth of the Singapore River and Sio Po (Small Town), better known as Kampong Glam. The area was predominantly Muslim in character and was the place where Bugis traders and immigrants came ashore. It is now one of Singapore's most historic areas and its name derives from the Glam tree (*Melaleuca leucadendron*) which provided its earlier inhabitants with a durable, slow-burning hardwood, bark for weaving and caulking boats, a fruit which gave a type of black pepper and whose leaves, when boiled and distilled, yielded cajeput oil. This was a popular rubefacient, used to treat minor aches and pains, sprains and rheumatism.

Kampong Glam was a boisterous neighbourhood. On one occasion, the Bugis, who were the main slave-traders, shocked Raffles by offering him a gift of a few slave-girls after auctioning fifty others and by 1820, when the 'native' population was deemed sufficiently large, two opium-shops were opened in the Kampong.[7] Some time later, a large trade in armaments was openly conducted in Kampong Glam and 'piracy was perfectly organised in Singapore'. The district became notorious for cockfighting and other forms of gambling, which greatly exercised the police and magistrates, to the concern of the expatriate community, who were daily informed by the press of frequent brawls, robberies, stabbings and murders.

Shortly after Burns's arrival, the *Straits Times*[8] reported that a party of 'Jolly Tars' from HMS *Iris* entered the house of a gentleman in that neighbourhood where he was entertaining friends 'employed on the light fantastic toe'. The sailors, who were intent on dancing a polka, seized a young lady as partner, 'which cast the ladies present into hysterics'. A fight ensued when 'the gallant gentlemen tried to expel the offenders' who were ultimately 'taken to the Police Station to dance the Polka or Hornpipe to their hearts content'.

But Singapore offered gentler diversions. Prints and water-colours of the town in the mid-nineteenth century show elegant military men in dress uniforms escorting ladies of fashion whose enemy is the sun. The scenes are redolent of Bournemouth, Brighton, Ryde or some other middle-class seaside resort, save for the apparent inertia, the lack of vitality and the sense of languid air, dense with humidity.

Naval and regimental bands gave regular concerts for the townsfolk and when HMS *Maeander* was in port, Captain Keppel 'kindly allowed its Band to discourse sweet music on the esplanade, of an evening.' When his ship was ordered to the China Station, Keppel's departure and that of his musicians were greatly regretted. However, the *Free Press* learned that *Maeander's* replacement, HMS *Hastings*, also had a band and 'we are sure that Captain Morgan only requires to have it hinted to him that the Singaporeans are musically inclined ... '[9] The Singapore Library flourished under a European committee of management and its acquisitions were regularly announced in the press. There were frequent dinners and soirées for the expatriates, interspersed with meetings of 'Zetland in the East', a masonic lodge that listed James Brooke and William Napier among its members. Then there was the stage!

The Theatre Royal, 'our little Drury', advertised 'laughable farces' and 'feats of Legerdemain and phantasmagorical displays' by Monsieur George, whose performances were sadly postponed in 1846 because they conflicted with the annual St Andrew's Day festivities. The London Hotel, which was acquired and renovated by Mr G. Dutronquoy early in 1839, was a popular rendezvous for local 'society' and overseas visitors, especially in 1850, when shipments of ice from North America were overdue. On that occasion, the proprietor offered fruit ices and ice wigs or caps 'at a rate so moderate as to place the luxury within the reach of many'. The ice-wig was a boon to invalids suffering from 'brain fever.'[10]

Those who favoured more strenuous pursuits played cricket on the Esplanade for 'Young Singapore' or the 'Military gents'. There was horse-racing, too, which became a biannual event, with riders competing in the 'big' race for the Governor's cup, valued at one hundred Spanish dollars. The more courageous hunted tiger and wild pig, although the former had the better of its encounters with the local inhabitants for many years. Swimming was not without attraction for some, but lost favour when a lad from the *India*[11] and later the cook from the *Ocean Queen* were taken by sharks in the harbour.

The *Straits Times* and the *Singapore Free Press* monitored the pulse of the new colony for readers of English, recording all events from amoks to the arrival of visiting clergy. They also carried the 'latest overseas intelligence' and when that was scarce, their columns contained anecdotes, sometimes humorous, sometimes sad, and at times frankly racist. In 1846, Singaporeans learned that:

> German physiologists affirm that of 20 deaths of men between 18
> and 25, ten originate in the waste of the constitution by smoking.

The news was even more disturbing in 1847 when it was reported that the fungal blight, which had destroyed the potato crops in Ireland and elsewhere, had precipitated famine in the Western Highlands and Islands of Scotland. The expatriate community responded immediately and with great generosity, enabling a local merchant, Mr W. W. Ker, to send a draft for the relief of 'the distressed Scotch and Irish'. However, by the time the money arrived, a substantial proportion was not required, because of the magnitude of charitable donations in Scotland and the rapid and efficient distribution of aid. A suggestion that the unexpected balance be given to the Royal Infirmary of Edinburgh, because of increased sickness following the famine, was unanimously accepted in Singapore[12] and the record of the benefaction still adorns the walls of the 'Surgical Corridor' in the main building. According to Mr Ker, that institution:

> ... is well known to every Scotchman as providing refuge, assistance
> and medical skill for sufferers under the combined misfortunes of
> poverty and sickness.

Readers were also reminded that cholera was not a malady confined to distant parts of the Empire. The disease reached Britain from India in the autumn of 1848 and was established in Edinburgh and its port of Leith in October of that year. On the night of 14 November the infection struck Glasgow in Springburn, close to the Forth and Clyde canal and when it apparently ceased, on 22 March 1849, 3,777 people were dead or 1.06% of the population of 355,800.[13] London was also affected, but the highly motile comma-shaped bacillus that causes the infection had yet to be discovered. However, as one correspondent to the *Singapore Free Press*, observed:

> You find a family suffering from cholera or fever and there is a filthy drain close by.

Punch, too, made serious comment when Brooke was honoured by the City of London.[14]

> We have not a word to say against Sir Peter Laurie's enthusiastic speech in honour of Mr Brooke, nor the heartiness with which the Common Council received his motion ... If Mr Brooke succeeded in his attempts to suppress piracy, Dr Lynch perished in his struggle with London fever. That 'to protect the oppressed, emancipate the slave and civilise the savage' is no nobler work than to succour the sick, toil for the suffering and enlighten the ignorant, – that the humanity which penetrates the jungle is twin brother to that which walks the hospital. No selfish motive impelled Dr Lynch any more than Mr Brooke; no avarice disgraced the conquest of the one over filth and fever, any more than those of the other over bloodshed and barbarity. The one triumphed, the other died in the struggle. The Common Council is justly eager to reward the victor, why should it hang back from honouring the martyr? Why should it not present the widow and orphan of Dr Lynch (Farringdon's martyr) with gold in another form?

Four years later the following stanzas appeared in the *Examiner*:

PAST AND PRESENT

A hint to Senators and Commissioners

London fell sick: ten thousand were struck down.
'Close every Churchyard! Empty every Drain!'
Were the loud cries throughout the trembling town;
Mayor, Meetings, Press, and Doctors swell the strain.

London got well. The cries then died away;
The danger past, the Sewers their ordure leak,
The grasping Rectors seize again their prey,
The Churchyards still with festering corpses reek,
And Thames, with poison well supplied from shore to shore,
Refunds its noxious stream, and is imbibed once more.

Anon.
Atheneum Club, Sept. 20, 1851.

Chapter VII

Antimony, Burns and Brooke

While Brooke was planning to return to England, Robbie landed in Singapore, solitary, unknown and without prospect of employment. But he had made a good friend in Captain Sinclair who allowed him to remain on board until the barque left for Bombay in mid-November. Sinclair knew the town well and was quick to inform his passenger of the small, but well-established Scots community, most of whom were traders or in shipping. However, Robbie needed little introduction; his arrival, like that of others, was published in the local press and gossip soon had it that he was indeed a relative of the Bard.

Sinclair mentioned the principal traders who advertised in the *Straits Times* and its rival, the *Free Press* and he advised Robbie to call in person. First, he had to find accommodation to suit his meagre purse and he chose to live in the Muslim quarter, Kampong Glam, where he was first listed as a resident in the *Singapore Almanack and Directory of 1848*. He could now devote all of his time to finding a job and he eventually made his way to Battery Road and the godowns of Hamilton, Gray – a trading company that opened in 1832. This was a shrewd undertaking by Glasgow merchants who anticipated the end of the East India Company's monopoly of commerce with India the following year. Robbie was received by an Indian clerk who offered to arrange a meeting with Mr Nicol, one of two Singapore-based partners in the company. Nicol, a Scot in his early thirties, had traded in Batavia before translocation to the exciting, new, free port.

This Aberdonian attained considerable prominence in Singaporean society. A staunch churchman, he proposed the toast to the 'Kirk of Scotland' at the St Andrew's Day dinner in 1843[1] and three years later, he chaired a meeting of 'Scotch Presbyterians' with the aims of forming a Presbyterian congregation in Singapore and finding a suitable minister.[2] There were so many 'Scotchmen' among the subscribers that the church was named St Andrew's. More than fifty years later, in Nicol's obituary, the *Singapore Free Press*[3] reported that 'it was a fad of his to invite Chinese Towkays and Babas to dinner and discuss with them various projects for the improvement of Singapore, among others that of the docks.'

Nicol also introduced the iron crane for use in the godowns and the first was installed on Boat Quay. The result was that 'four men could do three times as much work' than they could with the old-fashioned contrivance that served until the late 1840s.

'Come away in lad, out of this infernal heat!' Nicol shook Robbie's hand before immediately inquiring if it was true that he was related to the Poet. Burns was oddly unprepared for the directness of the question and stammered, 'He's my grandfaither.' This reply elicited a momentary feeling of uncertainty in Nicol: was his visitor telling the truth and did the canny Aberdonian detect a hint of Irish beneath Robbie's Glasgow dialect? The lad regained his composure, noting the fleeting light of uncertainty in Nicol's gaze, as he continued. 'Since my parents died, me and my brother have stayed with my sister. She's mairrit tae an Irishman.' Nicol appeared satisfied for the present and bade his clerk bring refreshment.

There were no immediate openings in the company, but Nicol recognised a kindred spirit in Robbie and the former's success intensified the youth's commercial aspirations. Nicol was clearly travelling on the high road to fortune. 'Have you heard of Borneo? Would you believe that Mr James Brooke became the Raja of Sarawak a few years back? A white Raja! Scarcely credible but it won't harm trade! I have a mind to write to my colleagues in Glasgow to see if they will support my proposal to send you to Bruné to explore prospects there. Brooke regularly ships the ore of antimony here and there may be other minerals. I have heard it said that gold is abundant. What do you say?'

Robbie was ecstatic, telling Nicol that he had enough money to live modestly in town and that he would try to see something of the region in the months before Nicol's receipt of a reply from Scotland. Furthermore, Captain Sinclair previously suggested the names of several ships based in Singapore and had surmised that Robbie might secure a free or discounted berth aboard one of the Honourable Company's steamers.

So young Burns joined a 'cruize' on 16 March 1847 aboard the *Hooghly*. Her course was first set for Malacca, an ancient port on the west coast of the Malayan peninsula and the ship's shallow draft allowed her to enter the river-mouth and tie up near the centre of the town. Robbie was so entranced that he was first ashore and immediately sought the Stadthuis, which he spied as the steamer steered a tight course up the narrow waterway. He was amazed to find that the town hall was two hundred years old, erected by the Dutch when they wrested the country from the Portuguese. Later during his stay, Robbie made his longer excursions in the relative cool of the evening, braving the mosquitoes that rose from the banks of the fetid river. Choosing Christ Church and its red laterite walls as a point of reference, he found Jonker Street and explored the labyrinth of narrow lanes in its neighbourhood. He greatly admired the facades of the red-roofed, two-storied houses that were home to the Baba community, the Straits Chinese, and he longed to stay in the cool inner courtyards occasionally glimpsed through partially open doors. On leaving harbour, *Hooghly* proceeded up the Straits of Malacca to the 'Pearl of the Orient', Penang. The steamer returned to Singapore on 29 April and six weeks later, Robbie set off for Labuan, en route to Brunei, to seek the Sultan's permission to travel to the interior.

Nicol's plan was deemed eminently worthwhile in Glasgow and the name, Robert Burns, did much to speed its appraisal. However, before Robbie left Singapore, Nicol was stern in his advice, especially where money was concerned. 'You must take great care in all of your transactions, particularly with 'that Prince of rogues, the Sultan!'

Labuan was Britain's most recent possession. This small island, some forty miles from Brunei, was formally annexed on 24 December 1846, less than a month after HMS *Iris* left Singapore 'carrying implements for cutting Roads, clearing jungles and a flagstaff ... ' She also transported 'a three-and-a-half foot length of granite to be placed on the highest part of the island'[4] proclaiming its impropriation by Queen Victoria. The island had been a notorious pirate base before becoming a pivotal centre for British traders in the nineteenth century, given its relative proximity to Hong Kong, Manila, Siam and Singapore. But one of the principal reasons for its acquisition was the recent discovery of coal, a potentially valuable resource in commerce and in war. Labuan was also the chief point of access to Borneo and it remains so today for those who spurn air travel.

The Sultan allowed Burns to go to Bintulu and ever alert to the occurrence of minerals, he noted customs and collected vocabularies of the Kayan dialects. He wrote that 'The coal and iron fields of the Balawi or Rajang are more extensive than any yet discovered on the Island ... Iron ore of a quality yielding from sixty to eighty per cent of iron abounds in the Baluwi or Rajang district ... over a district comprising nearly one half of the extreme breadth of the Island.'[5] He also discovered allegedly rich deposits of antimony and coal near Bintulu and he returned to Brunei to seek the Sultan's permission to work the mines. His Highness demanded a cash payment in advance.

Robbie returned to Singapore from Labuan on 23 September aboard the steamer *Nemesis*,[6] presumably to inform George Nicol and to seek financial support for the exploitation of his discoveries. His stay was short and he took passage for Borneo three and a half weeks later on the *Medea*.[7]

The granite slab erected in Labuan by HMS *Iris* on Christmas Eve 1846, now stands in Bandar Labuan (Labuan Town), formerly Victoria.

After a considerable delay, he reached Brunei on 15 January 1848 and closed negotiations with the Sultan and the Pangeran, Der Makota, before reporting to Hamilton, Gray.

However, on 5 January 1848, unknown to Burns, Brooke's deputy in Sarawak, Arthur Crookshank and Datu Patingi Ali, the Premier Chief, wrote to the Chiefs at Bintulu[8] informing them that people were trying to work the antimony ore at Bintulu. The translation read:

> We, Juan [sic] Crookshank and Datu Patingi, send this letter to the Chiefs at Bintulu to say that we have heard that there are people who are trying to work the antimony ore at Bintulu.
>
> Now we send this letter to say that the chiefs and people of Bintulu need not work the ore unless they like, and we know that they do not wish to open it. If, therefore, any persons (European or Malays) want to make them work against their will, do not work on any account if they do not wish, as no person can force or 'serra' them to do so.

Robbie was also seemingly unaware that the Sultan had already contracted to lease the exportation of antimony ore and tin to Mr W. A. Gliddon for a period of ten years 'from the Rivers of Bentooloo, Tatou and Balagnian'. When Gliddon and Company learned 'with much concern, that Mr Burns (backed by a large commercial house here) has subsequent to Mr G. leaving Bruni with his contract, obtained either an agreement or a letter purporting to give him the same privileges as those granted to G. & Co.', Perry, their representative in Singapore wrote to Rear Admiral Inglefield on 7 December 1847.[9] In this letter he offered proof of the priority of Gliddon's contract and stated the great injustice and breach of faith which would accrue to the Sultan should he conclude a similar agreement with Burns or any other party. The letter closed with the statement that 'Gliddon & Co, have been put to considerable expense during the last three months in bringing their agreement with the Sultan to its present stage'.

Meanwhile in Scotland, the Chairman of the Glasgow Chamber of Commerce, Walter Buchanan of Buchanan, Paterson and Hamilton, Gray, communicated with Lord Palmerston on 3 February,[10] praying that HM Government would not refuse their sanction to a lease granted by the Sultan of Bruné. The contract was that negotiated by Burns, although none of the British parties was mentioned by name. The Foreign Office replied that Viscount Palmerston was unaware of this grant and that the Chamber's petition would be referred to Brooke for information. However, it was stated that 'it may be a question of how far any undertaking of the kind could at present be carried on consistently with the personal safety of those who might be employed in conducting it.' The memorial was sent to Brooke on 23 February.

Burns returned to Bintulu in February 1848 with an escort provided by the Sultan and a letter from His Highness 'to the native chiefs of the country' confirming the concession. But Burns was unaware of a Treaty of Friendship and Commerce that had been agreed between the Sultan and Brooke in 1847, as he subsequently revealed in his letter to Lord Palmerston in 1851.

While Burns was engaged in negotiations and exploration in Borneo, his reports and those of others caused Nicol some anxiety and mounting displeasure. The *Straits Times* reported on 22 January 1848 that the *Zeelust* with Mr Gliddon, Superintendent of the Sarawak Smelting Company, had arrived at Singapore from Bintooloo, where it had anchored off the mouth of the river preparatory to visiting the antimony mines. But a shore party learned that a neighbouring chief was dead, that the people were foraying for heads and that they had best be off or be sacrificed, 'their heads being used to decorate the houses of the liege subjects of his dinginess the Sultan of Borneo!'

Burns reported to Nicol:[11]

Bruni, 14th February, 1848

Messrs HAMILTON, GRAY & Co.

In answer to your letter to the Sultan I trust that you will find the inclosed sufficiently explicit. Besides having the Sultan's chop it is attested by two of the most influential men of this place. The other paper is the duplicate of a letter from the Sultan to parties at Singapore, disclaiming any further communication with them regarding Bintulu, Tatow and Bulanian, the three districts contracted for by me. I received from Messers Guan Why, Teeang Why & Co. goods to the amount of dollars thirteen hundred and fifty, without which I found it impossible to proceed or accomplish my intentions with any degree of facility, the greater part of which I gave to the Sultan and part of the remainder to Macota. The rest I take with me to Bintulu. I arrived at Bruni on the 15th January and have been detained much beyond any expectation by the cursed procrastination of this people. But now I have got all in a fair way for starting and will leave I expect in the course of three or four days. The Sultan sends with me a Pangeran and letters to the Chief men at Bintulu which I have no doubt will ensure a favourable reception. I have sent you a sample of ore brought from a place to the North of Bruni. I am not aware of its properties but the person who gave it to me said it can be procured to a large extent.

Your most obedient servant
ROBERT BURNS

Nicol was more than a little annoyed when he replied to Burns.[12]

Singapore, 7th March, 1848

Robert Burns, Esq.
Bruni.

Dear Sir,

We received on the 25th ult. your letter of 14th ult. advising an order on us for goods bought from Tingwys Agent for $1,350, which after the positive instructions we gave you surprized us not a little. We particularly told you that in the mean time nothing must be done nor any money advanced at all events till the engagements of the Sultan were all completed, and we are sorry therefore to have to express our dissatisfaction at your overlooking our positive orders in such a way, and involving us at once in so large an advance as you have done. We cannot help saying you were very much to blame in the matter and we only hope now you will have been able to recover or make good part of the amount, as it is quite out of the question thinking for a moment of proceeding further, if we are to be exposed in this manner, to the risk of being drawn on without limit, without security and without prospect of any ultimate recovery or advantage. We fear you have allowed yourself to be deceived by the professions and delusive promises of the Sultan. The letter you sent us from the Sultan merely repeated what he before said – that nothing could be done till the Queen's answer was received ...

The report brought by the *Zeelust* is that the mines of Antimony are so far in the Interior that it is out of the question working them. This we know is merely a one sided statement, but it makes us apprehensive that you will find greater difficulties than you expected and till these were ascertained we think you were very wrong to make any outlay.

We by no means wish to damp your zeal or energies or to discourage you in any way. We are anxious to promote the scheme as far as we reasonably can, but we again entreat you and enjoin you not to advance a dollar more to any one without value received or till matters are finally settled between you and the Sultan ...

We hope you will be able to send us musters of Antimony and other Ores and of as many other productions, Mineral and Vegetable, as you can collect. The muster you sent us was Chlorite or Mica, of no value whatever ...

We repeat the advice we gave you verbally, do not be too sanguine in forming expectations or opinions, better to take a discouraging than too sanguine view of things.

G. G. Nicol

Ten days later, Nicol[13] wrote again to advise Burns that he had arranged for the *Auckland* to call at Bintooloo, to collect any freight and to instruct Burns to inform Makota that he wished to know the type of musical box he required. He added that if Burns wished to return, the *Corcyra* would provide a good opportunity. The correspondence continued in May[14] when Nicol informed Burns that the result of the application made to HM Government by 'our friends' at home concerning the Bintulu lease had been referred to Brooke. He also reproached Burns, stating:

... on no account advance a Dollar more as I was afraid nothing would be done or would be practicable. This I now confirm – from all that I have since learned from a Sambas Pangerang lately here of the Country of Bintooloo, I fear you have been too sanguine about the Antimony mines and that the obstructions to the navigation of the Bintooloo River will alone be too great an obstacle to overcome.

He added that Wise, now in Britain, had formed a new, chartered company for mining, trading and agricultural operations in Borneo, noting that:

This will be a further blow to your scheme and I fear you have now little chance, as there is no doubt that Mr Brooke will assist Mr Wise's scheme as much as he can and therefore oppose yours. This is a most barefaced scandalous job of Government and Mr Wise; and between the two the Sultan has been very ill used – when he assigned a grant of the Coal *to Government* he no doubt believed it was to be for the use and benefit of Government not of a joint stock Company …

The Sultan has a right to call on them to return the Grant and allow him to make his own terms or another arrangement with the Company or others. There is a strong feeling at home and here about this job and it would be well if you explained the matter to the Sultan and Moomin, and tell them that public opinion will support them in opposing the transfer of the Government Grant to a Company for monopolizing the Coal for their benefit in this way. The best plan would be for them to write me a letter stating that you had informed them of the establishment of the Company and that the Government had assigned to them the Grant of Coal, that the Sultan gave this Grant to the Queen's Government in good faith that it would be required and used exclusively for Government purposes – that if the Government does not use the Grant for themselves they should return it to the Sultan and let him make his own bargain with whomsoever is desirous of bargaining for it …

Such a letter as this might be very useful and I would lay it before the Commodore and Mr Brooke on their arrival. In my opinion such a Company as this, backed by Mr Brooke's influence, would do a great deal of harm rather than otherwise in Borneo, and would tend rather to check than increase trade with Bruni – point this out to the Sultan and the position it might place his authority in if a Company, powerful and privileged like this one, were allowed to settle in his dominions. Show him that it would be far better for him and his country to trust to private trade and individual enter-prize rather than large and monopolizing companies of this kind and explain to him that public opinion here and at home will support him in this; so he need not be afraid of incurring the censure of Government or any body.

Nicol concluded:

> I hope you will have brought back some produce of value against the Goods you took with you, otherwise there does not seem much chance of the $1,300 being got back again.

He also advised Burns again to look for Gutta Percha which would be 'far more valuable than Antimony'.

The result of Burns's negotiations in Brunei was published in the *Singapore Free Press* on 20 April which quoted a report in the *Courier* of 12 February that:

> Messrs Burns, Nichol [sic] and Lose, three gentlemen at Singapore, have obtained from the Sultan of Borneo, a lease for twenty years of the antimony mines at Bintooloo (to the northward of Bruni), for the sum of three thousand Spanish dollars annually. The effect of this will be to cut up Mr Brooke's monopoly at Sarawak and will reduce the price of Antimony at Sarawak, which Mr Brooke, by monopolis-ing, raised from 7 to 20 Sp.d. per cwt.

The paper also reported that Brooke had embarked at Portsmouth for Borneo on 31 March. He would not have been pleased to learn of Burns's coup.

Again, in Glasgow, Buchanan wrote to the President of the Board of Trade, as Chairman of the Chamber of Commerce, on 6 March.[15] On this occasion he expressed 'great surprise' at the public announcement that the Eastern Archipelago Company was to be incorporated by Royal Charter. Moreover, the shareholders were to enjoy limited responsibility and other exclusive privileges of trading with the Island of Borneo. The Scots also noted that:

> ... the trade contemplated by the projectors is of the most comprehensive description; and that the Merchants, Shipowners, Manufacturers and Coal-Masters of Glasgow and the surrounding districts are thereby threatened with a competition of the most unjust and ruinous nature.

The signatories requested that the President advise the Government not to grant the charter, nor to free the partners from unlimited liability, nor to confer exclusive privileges. In conclusion, the Glasgow Chamber wished to secure equal rights for all merchants and trading companies in every part of the East Indian Archipelago.

The response was swift and gave no quarter.[16]

> In the first place ... in the month of June last, Her Majesty was pleased to approve of a Charter incorporating the 'Eastern Archipelago Company' which Charter was accordingly issued, a few weeks after that date. At the same time, the nature and extent of its provisions and of the grounds upon which Her Majesty was advised to sanction it were to be afforded to the Directors of the Chamber of Commerce. The Company was incorporated for the limited period of twenty-one years with an initial capital of £200,000, capable of increase to £400,000 and above, with the consent of the Committee of Privy Council for Trade. No exclusive privileges other than those of incorporation were granted to the Company which was to conform to the directions of one of Her Majesty's Secretaries of State in respect of intercourse and dealings with foreign powers.

The objectives of the Company stated in the Charter were as comprehensive as the Glaswegians feared.

> The Directors of the Chamber of Commerce will perceive that the operations of the Company are intended to be limited to the newly established Colony of Labuan, and the adjacent Lands, which term is intended and understood to mean Borneo ... My Lords have not

lost sight of the principle, that the advantages of Incorporation and of the limited liability incident to it, should not, except in special cases, be conferred on Companies established for undertakings which may be carried on by individual enterprize;– but they were of opinion that the Case of the Eastern Archipelago Company was one of those special Cases.

It was considered that the resources of the new Colony of Labuan should be developed as quickly as possible, along with the opportunity of establishing new branches to trade with Borneo that arose through Brooke in Sarawak. The Lords also believed that these objects would be best promoted by the establishment of an incorporated Company with large capital exclusively applicable to these purposes. Such trade

> ... might be undertaken more safely, and with greater probability of success, and of the continuance of amicable relations with the native authorities, by a well-organized Company acting in a systematic manner, than by isolated enterprizes of private individuals.
>
> My Lords entertain a strong conviction that the existence and success of this Company will, so far from proving an obstacle to the progress of individual undertakings, be found to afford a valuable support to them.
>
> With regard to the objection offered by the Directors of the Chamber of Commerce, to the Governor of Labuan being a partner in the Company, – my Lords have not before them any fact shewing that any such partnership, direct or indirect, exists. My Lords, however, are confident, from the high character and disinterested conduct of that eminent individual, that there is no one to whom the protection and encouragement of the general interests of British Commerce in the Eastern Archipelago could be more safely entrusted that [sic] to Governor Brooke.

Chapter VIII

'The best laid schemes ... '

W hen Brooke returned to Singapore from England in May 1848, he replied to Palmerston's request for information concerning 'the working of the mineral productions in the district of Bintulu, Tatow and Balanian' under the lease granted to Burns.[1] He stated that the validity of the contract must rest on whether it was consistent with justice to the native population and if it could be carried out with safety to the parties concerned. Brooke also remarked:

> That the right of a Sovereign to grant the lease of the mineral pro-
> ductions of three large but unknown districts, without reference to
> the right of property vested in his subjects, is not quite so undoubt-
> ed and clear as the Chamber of Commerce seem to suppose.

He also wrote that it was debatable:

> ... whether the acquisition by individuals, for trading purposes, of
> such large and undefined rights over unknown districts, is at all
> desired or permitted; and whether an exclusive lease, if permitted,
> would lead at all to the general advantage of commerce.

Brooke then summarised the shortcomings of the Government of Bruné and reminded Palmerston of the character of the Sultan and the principal Pangerans, emphasising their complete inability to control the rivers and districts remote from the capital. He stressed that the districts of Tatow and Balanian were:

> ... inhabited by a wild population, so hostile and so entirely inde-
> pendent of Bruné, that no inhabitants of that city dare enter these
> rivers; and it would be certain death to any European who should
> attempt to do so under the auspices of the Sultan.

Brooke then made particular reference to the Kayan:

... a wild, warlike, hospitable [sic] race ... Such, my Lord, is a brief account of the districts in which Mr Burns proposes working the mineral productions, inhabited by a warlike and jealous population, in whose eyes at least he must appear as the agent of an oppressive Government ...

Brooke concluded by citing Gliddon's recent visit to the Bintulu River from which he 'was glad to escape with safety' and

... that any attempt to work the minerals of Bintulu would (independently of other objections) be attended with imminent danger to the parties concerned ... the increased facility of intercourse, the recent exemption of this people from oppression and misrule, the probability of the establishment of security for life and property, their very simplicity of character, the ordinary course of legitimate traffic, and the proximity of the new settlement of Labuan, must shortly lay open the resources of the Bintulu River, under proper regulations, to the enterprise of the British merchant ...

On the same day, Brooke wrote to the Hon E. J. Stanley of the Foreign Office.[2]

The Chamber of Commerce of Glasgow addressed a letter to me, a copy of which I inclose with my answer, which I think best to send through you to be forwarded or not as you may deem best.

It is the old question of parties rushing forward to gain profit, without any concern for the people of the country or the general advantage. For twenty years, the caution of the merchants here has outweighed their enterprise, and now their enterprise runs away with their prudence.

Brooke's response to Kinnear,[3] the Secretary of the Glasgow Chamber, was prefaced by the statement that confirmation of the lease granted by the Sultan of Borneo to Burns rested with HM Government and that he had merely been called upon to provide information on the subject. The content of this letter was essentially a summary of his remarks to Palmerston.

Brooke also met Nicol who wrote to Burns on 5 June[4] informing him of his conviction that:

> ... he is totally free from those desires to monopolise Borneo for his own benefit which some people imagined and may still imagine he has. I am quite satisfied he is actuated by the purest and highest motives and that his own personal interests in Sarawak are not for a moment considered by him.
>
> He does not and will not oppose your contract with the Sultan, on any other grounds than that there is an utter absence of any security for life or property in Bintooloo and the want of any valid title of the Sultan to the Territory – he says the Dyaks disclaim the Sultan's right and that they have expressed their determination not to allow his emissaries to go into their country or settle there. On these accounts and going as it were as an Agent of the Sultan, he thinks you have acted rashly as you run great danger of your life, especially as the Pangeran who has gone with you appears to be one of the deepest villains in Bruni, and would not hesitate to murder you for the sake of any little property you had (this Mr Low told me), and that at all events, till the sentiments of the British Government can be ascertained, it would be premature and might do mischief were you to remain longer in Bintooloo – he therefore suggests your leaving Bintooloo for the present, and I accordingly recommend you to do so. He has shown the most kind and friendly feeling and you will see volunteered to make search after you, fearing your life might be in danger. Being much alarmed at the possibility of any danger, which I did not before anticipate, I gladly accepted his offer and he is now to order the *Royalist* to make a search after you and which I trust will be successful. I have been, I can assure you, in a very anxious state of mind about you and now regret having had anything to do with the affair, particularly as it now appears the Sultan and others have been deceiving you by statements about the country; indeed it would appear that you have been much too sanguine and listened too credulously to all their plausible stories. You had better therefore give up all idea of any thing further just now. I only hope you will have been able to get some value for the money you so thoughtlessly gave away to the Sultan and Macota.

Mr Brooke thinks the Government at home will object to the Lease on the ground of the exclusive privileges you have got of Antimony. Be this as it may, I am quite sure you will meet with no interested or selfish opposition from Mr Brooke – discard from your mind all idea of this and take my advice, which is, to follow any suggestions or counsel he may give you, try to make a friend of him – you will find him I am satisfied willing to assist you by every means in his power as long as your conduct satisfies him, but do not think for one moment of thwarting him or acting in opposition to him – his power is now unlimited in Borneo. – Above all take care and don't commit yourself in word or deed with the Sultan or Macota – they are dangerous men and you will require to be very cautious what you are about.

Mr Brooke it seems has not only nothing to do with the Archipelago Company – *but is strongly opposed to it,* his wish is to encourage extension of trade in Borneo, but not by means of companies and monopolies of this kind.

He is going over himself in the *Meander* in about a month, you will judge for yourself whether you had best remain at Bruni or come back to meet him here.

He seems to think (as I have done for some time) that as a commercial speculation *you have been much too sanguine* – he says the expenses of working Antimony would be Immense, that Dyaks would never work, then that you must import Chinese at a great cost, that the mines are supposed to be at a great distance from the river, that the river is not navigable except for boats and altogether you have been going too much upon hearsay and the interested statements of the people of Bruni.

Mr Brooke is sending this by the *Phlegethon* to Sarawak, and I sincerely hope soon to have accounts of your safety, for I am very uneasy.

G. G. Nicol.

Brooke allayed Nicol's anxiety in a note and the latter communicated with Burns on 9 June:[5]

R. Burns, Esq.

My dear Sir,

Since I wrote you the other day I am happy to learn by the enclosed note from Mr Brooke of your safety at Bintooloo, but it seems now clear that the Sultan, like a rogue as he is, has duped you.

I think you had better do as Mr Brooke suggests – wait for him at Bruni, and I trust you will represent the injustice which has been done to you and us by the Sultan in exacting presents and money for a contract it is evident he had no power to sanction, and obtain Mr Brooke's influence to get a refund of the money or compensation of some kind. I am heartily sick of the business and not a little annoyed to think I have so foolishly been led into it and come under such a large advance. I trust to your earnest and energetic endeavour to get the money or its value returned and a word from Mr Brooke would I am sure accomplish it.

G. G. Nicol.

Three weeks later he wrote again[6] having learned from the *Auckland* that Burns was safe and well at Bintooloo.

I have nothing to add to what I have written, except that I shall be very glad to hear that you have got something at Bintooloo that will help to compensate for the money already so rashly expended, and you must not fail when Mr Brooke goes over to get his assistance if possible in demanding compensation for the money and goods exacted from you by the Sultan, under the false pretence that he had a right to the Bintooloo Territory which, it now clearly appears he has not ...

I hear that the Kayan Chiefs express their willingness to open the Bintooloo, Baram and all other Rivers to trade, provided Mr Brooke will promise his protection which of course he will do. They all say that the quantity of wax, camphor &c. there is immense, so you may still have a good field before you without Antimony, which I never thought much of ...

The vexed Nicol continued his exhortations:[7]

Singapore, 23rd July, 1848.

Robert Burns, Esq.

My dear Sir,

I have been waiting from time to time in the expectation of letters from you, but up till now have been disappointed, doubtless you had no certain opportunities at Bintooloo, but it is a pity you did not try the chance of writing by native boats. Our last dates from Bruni are 1st July. These have brought an extraordinary report of your having been married to the daughter of the Dyak Chief at Bintooloo. I thought it was a joke but on sending for a Malay Nacodah from Bintooloo who came over in the *Amelia*, he told me that it was true and that you had been married to the daughter of Akumlassa, the Kayan Chief. This is a piece of intelligence which I certainly was not prepared for, but of course it is an affair I have nothing to do with. I hope only it may strengthen your position, which I should think it likely to do. The Nacodah told me he was the bearer of a letter from Akumlassa to Sir James Brooke asking his protection and advice, and expressing a wish for him [Brooke] to go to Bintooloo – he is going to Bintooloo as I told you, and now I suppose it is likely you will not return to Bruni, so that you may see Brooke at Bintooloo.

We hear also that you are getting plenty Antimony Ore. I hope this may be true, but on the other hand I hear you are likely to pay very high for it from the difficulty of transporting it and the distance. If so you will likely do little good with it as I repeat to you, what I have often told you, that unless Antimony Ore can be got for little more than the cost of putting into boats it will never do any good ...

I myself have little faith in this Antimony, at all events I hope you may be able soon to send some of this or other produce over to reduce the outlay already incurred. Our friends in Glasgow are dissatisfied with you for drawing on us so large a sum as you did, and I would be very glad to see this squared off.

Your new position as regards Akumlassa will of course alter your relations to Sir James Brooke and the Sultan – as regards the latter the lease of course and the annual payment fall to the ground

– it is clear he has and had no more right to Bintooloo than he had to Java and you must try as I told you to recover through Sir James Brooke what he exacted from you on the false pretence of his rights over Bintooloo. – With respect to Sir James you will be placed in a delicate position, he maintained from the first that the Sultan had no authority over Bintooloo and that Akumlassa alone held sovereign rights over it, now as this Chief and you have come to an under-standing Brooke of course can have no ground for objecting to your settlement there ...

If Akumlassassa [sic] has given you rights and entered into agreements with you and if he is anxious you should remain at Bintooloo, you will not allow other considerations to interfere against this to your own disadvantage, or what may seem to you so, – on the otherhand it would be bad policy to run counter to Sir James Brooke's views. *I am convinced his motives are pure and free from all selfishness or desire to aggrandize his power and personal influence. I think therefore your wisest course, as I have before told you, is to act in friendly concert with him.* Whatever your eventual posi-tion may be in Bintooloo, he has and will have it in his power to be of essential service to you, and you will gain much more credit and strength by attaching yourself to him than by attempting to act counter to his views. This is my own opinion only, – I do not ask you to act upon it against your own, but I advise you to reflect well before you embark on any course of policy which may bring down upon you Brooke's opposition ...

It is true some foolish people about him have been I hear utter-ing some dark hints about Englishmen going to Bintooloo being left to have their throats cut without the British Government interfering – or something to this effect. I do not know that you *have* any right to claim any such protection, but I am quite sure Sir James Brooke is not the man to withhold it whatever the people about him may say. *When he thought your life in danger he volunteered to make enquiries about you* – he has evidently been in error about the dan-ger you incurred, as it appears you have met with a friendly recep-tion – so the Nacodah says – This man by the way says that Tin Ore abounds in Bintooloo. If combined with this you can command a supply of Coal, Tin is far more likely to repay you than Antimony ...

There was still no news from Burns by late August so Nicol wrote again[8], cautioning him 'about Antimony as a speculation' and the 'qualities' of Bornean Gutta Percha which 'are worthless'. He also mentioned that Brooke had called on him before leaving on *Meander* and said that:

> ... he will willingly give you all the protection in his power ... I advise you very strongly to lean to him, to attach yourself to him and gain his confidence by every means in your power. You cannot do this more effectually than by making the position you have acquired subservient in carrying out his public views and measures ...
>
> He said that he thought the British Government would not sanction your exclusive right to Antimony. I told him that I myself was not friendly to any exclusive rights of this kind – now that the Lease of that prince of rogues the Sultan is cancelled; as of course it is. I advise you to have nothing to do with exclusive rights or privileges of any kind, let trade and all other pursuits be as free as possible and do not seek for yourself any advantages which are denied to others ...
>
> In the position you have now acquired for yourself you require no fictitious advantage of this kind, you will always have natural advantages which ought to suffice and satisfy you ...
>
> I asked you to try and recover what the Sultan exacted from you on the grossly false pretence of his rights over Bintooloo and to account of the annual payment for the Lease. Perhaps Sir James may object to interfere and say it is your own fault trusting him. I am excessively annoyed at your having allowed him to swindle us in such a way, but if you discover from what Sir James Brooke says that he is not likely to interfere, or that it may place you in an unpleasant position towards him, you can avoid the subject and wait for some better opportunity. I am anxious on your own account that you should do nothing to disturb the good feeling with which he is prepared to receive you.
>
> G. G. Nicol

Robbie at last wrote to Nicol on 4 September[9] apologising for his lack of communication which was due 'in great measure' to his having had 'to conform to circumstances.'

On my reaching Bintulu and finding the state of things relative to the lease so different to that which I was led to believe previously to going there, I was left but the choice of two ways, either to return without ascertaining definitely how matters stood or to remain and find out as I best could. The latter way I tried, which caused me so much delay, and being the greater part of the time in the interior of the country, I had not a single opportunity of writing you, nor of hearing from you before the *Phlegethon* arrived at Bintulu on the 2nd of August. I was then only a few days returned from the Kayan country, where I had went after having examined the Antimony, learning that it did not belong to the Sultan, but to the Kayan. I made a bargain with them, of which the enclosed is a copy. I returned to Labuan in the *Phlegethon* and received your letters. Since then I have been waiting to meet Sir James Brooke here. I have just returned after being ten days in Bruni. I found them very plausible, the Sultan was anxious to pay for the Goods he had from me, but at a disadvantage I could not comply with. I therefore thought better to leave it so until Sir James Brooke arrives – after meeting him I intend returning as soon as possible, and until then I will not attempt giving you the details of my proceedings at Bintulu, as I trust it will then be satisfactory to you after having ascertained all that I possibly could on the subject. I was sorry to perceive that you were misinformed regarding my having got a quantity of Antimony ready, though I was received in a friendly manner at all the places I went to and found the people available for any kind of work, I done nothing further than instructing them to gather Gutta Percha and other kinds of produce against the coming of a vessel ...

A further letter on 26 September[10] informed Nicol that Burns had not recovered sufficiently from an attack of fever which had prevented his copying his earlier correspondence sent by the *Amelia*. Brooke was expected daily, but his delayed arrival and the prevalence of fever were 'much against the new colony, indeed from its present state success must be doubtful for sometime to come'.

Nicol replied on 1 November[11] with the hope that Burns had recovered and recommended him 'to be careful' of himself.

There is little in your letter per *Amelia* calling for notice now. Till you come over or send more explicit information it would be useless offering any opinion on the contract you have made with the Kayan Chief. I have often told you and repeat that you do wrong to lay so much stress on Antimony ore, and I repeat also my opinion that you injure yourself by aiming at exclusive right and monopolies; the position you have gained is enough to secure for you all the advantage you need desire if any thing can be done at all, which remains to be seen. I am glad to see you are turning your attention to Gutta Percha. This promises to be of infinitely greater importance than Antimony Ore.

I hope you have succeeded in recovering from the Sultan the value of the Goods he so unscrupulously cheated you out of. I hope this will be a lesson to you to be less credulous hereafter of promises and professions of such people.

G. G. Nicol.

Chapter IX

Burns, Explorer and Ethnographer

On 5 October 1848, the *Straits Times* and the *Free Press* reported that Robbie had arrived in Labuan from Bintulu and Brunei, noting that he had amassed an abundance of antimony ore at Bintulu. He was suffering from 'fever' and the *Times* was unaware if he intended to settle permanently at that place or not.

When Robbie disembarked at Labuan, he was bone-weary, profoundly anaemic and so weak that he could scarcely walk ashore unaided. Each intermittent attack of fever left him more physically and mentally impaired, but he rallied sufficiently to return to Singapore on 16 November on board the *Royalist*.

He at once called on Nicol, 'having cancelled the bargain with the Sultan' and obtained a refund of part of the advance from Hamilton, Gray. Still weak, Robbie was wholly unprepared for his employer's impending verbal assault.

'At least you're safe', were Nicol's only words of welcome. 'You had better sit'.

Robbie was glad of the invitation as his poor health seemed to make him unduly sensitive to the heat and humidity. He had also dreaded this encounter.

'You are far too sanguine, as I have repeatedly told you. Why did you not heed my advice? Have you no sense, man? I have to account for all the money that you have so foolishly squandered and I must accept responsibility for your misdeeds. After all that I have done for you! I was the first to hold out a friendly hand when a friendly hand was needed and contrary to the advice of more than one party. It was I who supplied you with funds to assist you to carve out your own success. Look at how you've repaid me! Mr Low told me that you behaved abominably at the Sultan's court and were fortunate that he did not exact your miserable life. And what of my firm? It was respected before you brought it into disrepute. What will Glasgow make of this? I have finished with you, finished, do you hear?'

Robbie tried to mount a defence. The continual procrastination at

Brunei, his ignorance of protocol and the fever had so heightened his frustration that he had finally lost control. He had wanted to die but Nicol had none of it.

'Die, did you say? You were within an inch of being stabbed to death. Had the Sultan not been in fear of Sir James, as he now is, you would not be here today.'

Robbie heard Nicol as in a dream. He seemed curiously detached from his body in which every bone ached and each muscle screamed in agony. Even his thoughts entered his mind like flights of darts from Kayan blowpipes. He had no response. Defeated and dejected, he crawled to his lodging and instantly collapsed into a deep and dreamless sleep.

Hours later, he awoke somewhat refreshed, counted his money and resolved to continue trading, but in his own right. He first consulted Mr Woods, the Editor of the *Straits Times* and one of Brooke's most outspoken critics in the region. They had met socially, shortly after Robbie first landed in Singapore, and admiring the young man's courage, Woods was generous in his advice. He was fascinated by Robbie's adventures in Borneo and introduced him to the Editor of the *Journal of the Indian Archipelago and Eastern Asia* that first appeared in June the previous year. Robbie's proposal to write on the exploration of Kayan country was received with enthusiasm and alacrity and he was promised every assistance in his preparation.

The papers were published in 1849[1,2] to editorial acclaim in the journal which was launched for the literary and scientific interests of British residents in those parts. The monthly issue was highly regarded but is now, sadly, long defunct.

Robbie was the first European to visit Kayan territory and he did so in 1848 to assess its 'productions and capabilities'[3] and to determine if its inhabitants would welcome contact with Europeans. He travelled first to Bruni, in the accepted belief that the Sultan held sway in those regions, and was permitted to ascend those rivers that gave access to the Kayan.

At that time the territory between the Baram and Bintulu rivers was not part of Sarawak and although it lay within the sovereignty of Brunei, it was populated and controlled by the Kayan. The Kayan had a fearsome reputation as warriors and Burns attributed their independence and superior power in part to their knowledge of manufacturing iron and steel from local iron ore. Indeed, Robbie claimed that the Kayan made 'better iron than that of England'.

Topographically, the Baram country consists of three regions; a lowland plain with meandering rivers, dense forests and swamps; an intermediate expanse of hilly, broken country with forest and a high plain surrounded by mountains. The Baram river with its main tributaries flows north to discharge into the sea close to the border between Sarawak and Brunei. In 1848, Hugh Low[4] estimated that the Kayan in the region exceeded 270,000 and that this was a conservative figure, because the tribes attempted to evade payment of a head-tax imposed by their Malay rulers. These numbers had dwindled to about 7000 by the early 1970s.

In his laudatory introduction to Burns's first paper, the Editor[3] concluded a summary of the young man's travels by stating that:

> All difficulties, real as well as imaginary, in the way of research in the Archipelago, vanish before an enterprising and indefatigable spirit like that which enabled Mr Burns to explore the country of the Kayans, without any assistance or protection from either the English colonial governments or the Sultan of Borneo ...

Robbie first spent seven days negotiating the Tatau which disgorges into the South China Sea, some ten miles southwest of the estuary of the Bintulu; there he encountered Kayans in the upper reaches. On his return to the coast, he ascended the Balinian and after exploring this river, Robbie started up the Bintulu where he reached Taban, the first Kayan village, fifty miles upstream at its bifurcation. He then followed its northern branch to within a short distance of the Kayan of Baram. After retrieving his route to Taban, Robbie travelled up the other branch in an easterly direction until he reached its source two days later. He then struck eastwards through the jungle until he arrived at night at the Balaga, a large tributary of the Rejang. Two days later he reached its confluence with the great river and the village of Balaga, whose chief was Lasa Kalan. After two further days upstream, Robbie descended as far as Langkoho and met the chief Akam Knipa before continuing below the Great Rapids of the Rejang, now known as the Pelagus Rapids. There he came to the village of Tanjong and by ascending the Palawi, a feeder of the Rejang, he reached the Tatau and descended to the coast. Including travelling time, Robbie spent three months among the Kayan and six months in their vicinity.

Burns's first paper, entitled 'The Kayans of the North-West of Borneo', opens with a topographical description of Kayan territory, detailing its extent and boundaries with particular reference to the Rejang river which:

> ... is navigable as far as the influence of the tide, which flows to the foot of the Great Rapids, a distance of from ninety to an hundred miles. The rapids are fully two miles in length ...

Burns then enumerates the wild animals and comments on the peoples:

> ... the rhinoceros is the largest, and is found about the upper parts of the Rajang, where also the largest species of orang utan is said to exist ... The configuration of the country does not vary more than do its human inhabitants. Besides the mongrel Malays of the coast, there are eleven other tribes located between them and the Kayans ...

and he describes how the first six listed by him 'have all sprung from the one called Kanowit ... '

As with other early papers, Burns uses some place names 'which it is now impossible to place with certainty', wrote Harrisson in 1951.[5]

> Most of his spellings are, however, unusually accurate and still valid. It is clear that he must have actually been up the Rejang past the great Pelagus Rapids – to this day the obstacle to commerce which he prophesied over a century ago – to Belaga and probably beyond, before any other outsider.

Similarly, he was the first to recognise the low density of the population in the interior and Harrisson concluded that:

> The paper, though short and in the generalised amateur character of

its time, contains many other points of great interest for comparison today, – on burial, clothing, language, trade, sexes etc ... This paper is a unique document. Not until more than thirty years later did Brooke Low (1882) give another good description of these inland people. By then great changes had already taken place. Without this document we should never be able to reconstruct the pattern of the past in important ways which, through Burns, are preserved.

Robbie's description of his initiation as a blood brother of a Kayan chief merits quotation in full because in it, as in the rest of the paper, he reveals his honesty, humanity and keen powers of observation.

None of the other tribes of the Island seem to practise the strange but not singular custom, of one person becoming the friend or brother of another, by the blood of each being mingled and partaken of mutually, either by drinking, or smoking. By the former mode, Mr Dalton describes his having become the friend of a Kayan chief of the Coti river. Amongst the Kayans of the northwest the ceremony is somewhat different. The following was observed on my initiation into the brotherhood with Lasa Kulan, the chief of Balaga on the Rajang, and of Tubow on the Bintulu river. Two days previous to that on which the bloody affair came off, the great hall of the chief was garnished with the weapons and gaudy skin war dresses of the men, and dashed with a fair sprinkling of the finery of the women kept more for show than use. On the day appointed, a number of the neighbouring chiefs having arrived, several of them commenced proceedings by haranguing on the greatness and power of their ownselves, and of all the wonders they had heard of the white people, and of their satisfaction in being visited by one of them, of whom their fathers had heard so much but had never seen. Next a large pig provided for the occasion was killed, the throat-cutting part of the business being performed by one of the fair sex, seemingly with great satisfaction to the attendant crowd of men. Next were brought three jars full of arrack of three sorts, severally made from rice, sugar-cane, and the fruit tampui. In pieces of bambu it was dealt out in profusion to all present, the ladies excepted.

On the chief taking a bambu filled with arrack, we repaired to the balcony in front of the house, and stood side by side with our faces towards the river. The chief then announced his intention of becoming the friend or brother of a son of the white man, on which one of the attending chiefs gave me a small sharp pointed piece of bambu with which I made a slight incision in the right fore-arm of the chief, and the blood drawn was put on a leaf. The chief then with a similar instrument drew blood from my left fore-arm, which was put on the same leaf and mingled with the other. The blood was then mixed with tobacco and made up into a large cigar which we puffed alternately until it was finished, when my new friend delivered himself of a long and eloquent speech invoking their god Tanangan, the sun, moon, and stars, and rivers, the woods and mountains to witness his sincerity. Three times during this declamation, he sprinkled the arrack on the ground towards the river. My speech, being delivered, several of the principal chiefs present held forth both long and loud enough. We afterwards returned to the hall and the cheering beverage went round more merrily than before, calling forth their good nature and social disposition. Although no toasts were given, still each successive bumper was accompanied by a merry and noisy chorus. The feast came afterwards, and the whole affair was wound up by music and dancing which lasted until about midnight. The varied war dances of the men were amusing, the slow and measured pacing of the women monotonous, but still far from ungraceful.

Robbie remained in Borneo and on 12 July 1848, the *Straits Times* reported that it learned from the arrival of the *Amelia* that he had collected 'an abundance of antimony ore' at Bintulu and that he was 'said to be doing well'. Three days later the paper stated that:

> ... it must be gratifying to learn that while the development of the mineral resources of Borneo proper promise an enlarged supply of antimony ore, its extended use in the arts offers encouragement to the speculator, and promises a steady demand at remunerative rates.

There followed a report of a recent meeting of the Liverpool

Polytechnic Society where a Mr Forrest described the use of the 'white oxide of antimony' in a paint superior to that based on white lead and at half the cost.

In addition to news of Burns on 5 October 1848, the *Singapore Free Press* gave out that the *Auckland* had brought a report from Labuan of 'considerable fever prevailing in the Colony, and amongst the shipping in Victoria Harbour and at Bruni ... ' The paper also stated that 'the prolonged non-arrival of the Governor and other members of Government, had caused considerable disappointment and would retard the progress of the colony'.

However, Brooke and his suite were in the course of a 'Royal' progress at Sarawak where he assured the European inhabitants that his feelings towards the country were unchanged. He also presented each of the three principal Datus with a valuable sword, pledging that he and Keppel would protect them, 'whilst the most active measures would be taken against the pirates'. After the ceremony, Pangeran Mahomed and most of the native chiefs were given a trip on the *Ranee*, a sixty-foot steam gun-boat 'of elegant proportions' designed by *Maeander's* Ship's Carpenter[6]. Built of teak in Singapore, coppered and copper-fastened, this little boat had a beam of eight and a half feet and drew twenty-six inches, when fully manned and armed. However, at her launch on 14 August 1848, 'those conversant with steam and navigation' deemed that her four horse-power engine was wholly inadequate for the purpose.

The day after the festivities in Sarawak, at the request of the inhabitants, Keppel embarked his splendid brass band on board the *Ranee* and the populace was entertained, as the graceful little steamer glided along the bright waters of the Sarawak river. However, it was noted that:

> ... some of the most popular airs, amongst which was the 'Sarawak Polka', lately introduced from England, failed to produce amongst the swarthy assembly that devotion to the shrine of Terpsichore, which it did on its first introduction into the ball-rooms of old England.

Maeander got under weigh on 29 September 1848 and Brooke first set foot on Labuan as Governor on Monday 2 October, a day proclaimed as a general holiday. All the European inhabitants were requested to appear at Government House to hear Her Majesty's Commission, and a detachment of Keppel's marines was landed with the ship's band and marched to the Esplanade for evolutions.

The celebrations were short-lived. The *Straits Times* of 4 October reported that 'Fever' had prostrated most of the persons who had lately resorted to Labuan and that there were several deaths. On the 25th the same paper stated that 'malignant fever' had occurred in the new colony which was 'fast becoming the graveyard of those who resort to it'. There was also scurvy among the crew of the *Royalist*. One day later, in a letter to Templer, Brooke[7] penned that:

Fever has struck us all, the greater number are miserable weak shadows, and the worst of it is that no sooner does one recover, than another is attacked ... It is a very strange and remarkable fact in this fever, that though all have been attacked, it has only proved fatal to the lower class of Europeans, and to the Chinese, whilst the better class of Europeans have been rarely dangerously ill, and not a single death has occurred amongst them, whilst the same held good with the Malays and natives of India, the Chinese alone being sufferers. This I have no doubt arises from the debauched habits of our seamen and marines, and of the Chinese, and in many, probably most cases, other causes have supervened upon the fever, to produce a fatal result.

The day after Brooke returned from Brunei in *Maeander's* steam tender, the *Ranee*, the monsoon struck with full force and the sea rose to an unprecedented height, sweeping over the beaches, flooding houses and damaging stores. The accompanying rain which was prolonged and violent, inundated the swamps around Victoria harbour creating a huge pool of fetid water.

Robbie announced his intention of returning to Singapore as soon as possible after meeting Brooke, to acquaint Nicol with all the facts and he wrote to Nicol from Labuan on 5 November[8] stating that after waiting so long for the event, 'the Governor has went to Brunei at last.' Burns travelled with him and was paid for goods purchased by the Sultan and Pangeran Makota, Brooke's 'greatest enemy'. His reception by Brooke was straightforward and more agreeable than he had expected and Burns was 'kindly offered his assistance as far as in his power.' Burns also informed Nicol that he had further delayed his return to Singapore because of another bout of fever, but that he intended accepting Lieutenant Gordon's offer of a passage in the *Royalist*. He arrived on 16 November, aboard the schooner which had been taken under tow by the Honourable Company's steamer *Auckland* and five days later, the *Straits Times* noted that four patients with fever of a severe type were sent to hospital before the *Royalist* was towed to Trincomalee in Ceylon for a refit.

Six weeks before, *Royalist*, under the command of Lieutenant Gordon, left Labuan for Singapore. The following day:

> ... the wind blew strong from S.W. and freshened towards night; in the morning it blew a gale and the ship rolled fearfully, so much so that the sea made clean breaches over the vessel, the water finding its way down the gun-room hatch. The sails reefed according to the gale, and the day was got through miserably enough. At 8 pm it became very squally; as night advanced, it was found necessary to take a treble reef in fore-topsail, which with fore topmast staysail and spanker was all the canvas the *Royalist* dare show to the elements. Daylight of the next day brought no abatement of the gale: the vessel sped her course on the wings of the wind. By noon (Oct. 5th) the *Royalist* was about 30 miles to the N.W. of Tanjong Barram – the wind still continuing its fury and the sea lashed into foam. At 11 pm a squall occurred, sudden and violent, and took the ship aback, but she soon again paid off; the officer of the watch continued shortening sail: had the mainsail up, spanker scandalized, and was engaged forehead hauling the jib down – the vessel rushing through the foam at the rate of 6 or 7 knots. – At this critical juncture, the foresail took itself in by the tack, being carried away, when another gust took her. The hands were stationed by the topsail halyards, but before these could be let go a third gust took the ship aback: in board went the bowsprit, down fell the main-topmast, overboard went the foremast, crash went the main-mast carrying away the mizenmast, quarterboats and dingy, and splintering the wheel to atoms, in a moment converting the prim *Royalist* into a perfect wreck.

But amidst such a scene of broken wreck not a man was injured – all were providentially saved. The terrific crash was followed by a suspense truly awful. The ship was now staggering, each successive sea pouring down the hatchways, and everything betokening the vessel's descent into the mighty deep.[9]

The crew cleared the wreck and by 10 a.m. next day *Royalist*, making four knots under jury rig, was able to limp into Labuan, accompanied by *Meander*.

On 28 November Keppel logged that the whole of Labuan was down with fever, many of his marines were ill and a large number had died. Brooke was not immune, and fearing for his life, Keppel removed him to isolation in *Maeander*, where the sick lay in cots on both sides of the main-deck. By mid-December, the graveyard on Labuan 'was filling up in a manner to excite alarm' and the new colony had lost fifteen percent of its population from disease in less than five months. There is no doubt that the decision to settle the swamps around the harbour was a potent factor in the aetiology of 'Labuan fever' and Brooke resolved to relocate the residences and barracks to higher ground, before draining the marshes.

The death toll rose; a Mr Burns from Hong Kong, who visited Labuan with a view to settling there, succumbed and Lieutenant Gordon, the *Royalist's* popular Scots Captain died of the infection in Singapore on 1 December 1848, at the age of twenty-eight.[10] Most of the European community attended his funeral.

Five years on, Labuan's notoriety as a 'graveyard' for all who 'resorted to it' had not diminished nor had Brooke's unpopularity receded. 'An Unhappy Resident' of the island colony expressed his opinion in the *Straits Times* on 15 March, 1853.

Dear Sir,

I would feel much obliged by the insertion of the accompanying lines in your excellent journal.
They are descriptive of a British Colony not 1000 miles away, and their correctness is generally acknowledged.
Leaving you and your readers to guess the locality of the said colony.

Yours etc.'

The Model Colony.

A noble House his Honor founds
Which costs the Queen 4000 pounds
And grants the sum of 38
To make and mend the Colony.
Tis thus, forsooth, we do hehold
How poor John Bull is bought and sold:
In fact we also see the way
Economy is made to pay.

A well paid chief , a motley crew
Of Underlings, entirely new
To bus'ness; whose former trade
Has taught them how to use a spade,
To polish boots, to act as Quacks
Or preach a sermon to the Blacks;
Their number is (no need of guesses)
One to each man who land possesses.

An undrain'd plain, some stumps of trees
A red tiled House, the eye to please,
Where sit the Beaks with Peons and Bums,
Waiting for work which seldom comes;
And when it does, to suit their ends,
They cheat their foes to serve their friends;
A flag staff with a gilded crown,
Some stinking pigsties called "the Town."
No road to drive a Buggy;
And at a glance you quickly see
Our new and model colony.

Explanation, if it is required: 'His Honor' – Title of Lieut. Governor. Grant for 1853 in model Colony 4000 pounds for Government House. – The only House in the place (and no road to it as yet. 33 pounds for roads, drainage etc., etc. An undrain'd plain is a swamp where the Inhabitants of 'The Town' live, or more properly die.

Chapter X

Burns, the Sultan and Brooke

W hen Burns first sailed to Borneo in the *Amelia,* Gliddon, the Superintendent of the Sarawak Smelting Company, was there attempting to negotiate a lease from the Sultan to mine the minerals in the Bintulu region. According to Hugh Low,[1] who minuted a conversation with Pangeran Makota aboard the latter's boat, Gliddon's intentions were strongly opposed by Pangeran Moumein with the result that the lease, drawn up by Gliddon, was never confirmed by the Sultan or Makota. Some time later, Robbie obtained a grant, but only the Sultan's chop or seal was attached to it because Moumein remained opposed. When the naval Commander-in-Chief, Admiral Inglefield, arrived, the matter was referred to him by Burns, and the Pangeran explained to the Admiral that if the lease was confirmed 'he wiped his hands of the whole affair, and left the responsibility with the Admiral and the Sultan.' On hearing this, Inglefield gave no opinion, although 'he thought it was right of the Pangeran to wait until he had an opportunity of consulting Sir James Brooke, or communicating with Her Majesty's Government.'

Once the Sultan's private seal was affixed to his document, Robbie gave the Sultan goods to the value of over eight hundred dollars in a private transaction, outwith the knowledge of Pangeran Moumein who was apprised of it later. The terms of this advance were that Burns was to travel to Bintulu with a Pangeran in one of the Sultan's boats and there he was to inspect the country and search for minerals. Furthermore, provided Robbie worked the mines or found them capable of being worked, the cost of the goods given to the Sultan was to be part of the first stipulated payment. But if no minerals were found or if they could not be exploited, the Sultan was to pay for the goods within six months.

There were delays in readying the boat for Bintulu and Robbie feared for the completion of his contract, so he asked Moumein to stand surety for the amount of the goods. Moumein agreed, 'for the credit of the Sultan, and to preserve something like quietness', because Robbie had become very troublesome, addressing the Sultan and the Pangerans in such violent and abusive terms that all were eager to get rid of him. A boat was procured and Pangeran Alludeen was appointed to take Robbie to Bintulu, but a close relative of Alludeen's, a child, became unwell, precipitating further delay. Robbie, who became extremely angry and unusually violent, went to the Palace and called the Sultan 'by such opprobrious epithets and used such threatening gestures, standing while he spoke, that the Sultan retired from the apartment'. Makota informed Hugh Low that had the Sultan and his nobles not been in fear of the English, Burns would not have left the hall alive.

The boat with Robbie and Alludeen left Bruné the following day, but by the time they had reached the mouth of the river, the crew had so resented Burns's violent conduct, that all but three jumped ship. Alludeen had forgotten or feigned to bring any gunpowder so he returned to Bruné, saying that he would come back next morning, but when he did not reappear at the appointed time, Robbie grew angry, jettisoned a quantity of sago and other provisions and got the boat under weigh with the remaining crew. A contrary wind forced him to Labuan, where unfavourable weather constrained him to anchor. In the meantime, Alludeen had returned to where he left Robbie after spending two days at Bruné, only to find no trace of the boat, so he left immediately to inform the Sultan and Pangeran Moumein. After some days, news arrived of Burns's position and Moumein escorted Alludeen to the boat and provided a new crew. The voyage was completed without incident, except for Robbie's outbursts. Makota told Low that from what he knew of Alludeen's character, it was a wonder that Burns was not summarily killed, but Alludeen had been severely cautioned in Bruné.

On arrival at Bintulu, Robbie and the Pangeran resumed their feud and after spending some time in that region, Robbie went inland to Kayan territory where he spent several months. Upon his return by way of Labuan he demanded repayment from the Sultan, who offered goods as he had no money. Burns refused them, alleging that they were of insufficient value and he abused the Sultan and his court on more than one occasion, threatening the vengeance of Sir James Brooke and the English. This frightened the Sultan and he promised to repay Robbie, having heard that he was to receive money from the Government of Labuan at the end of October, when Burns accompanied Brooke to Bruné. However, once the sum was in the Sultan's hands, he procrastinated, despite Robbie's repeated tantrums which Hugh Low[2] witnessed on one occasion: I 'thus had to see the accredited agent of a large mercantile firm so totally devoid of temper, and conduct himself in so reprehensible a manner, and wreck, by his uncontrollable passion, the very interests which he wished to serve.' Again, only the fear of Brooke and the English prevented Burns's violent death.

The Sultan[3] then wrote to Brooke and informed him of the contract with Burns who said that the ore could not be worked because it was a long way inland. The Sultan stated that he did not wish to enter into any further engagements with Burns, but he had heard that the latter wished to return to Bintulu. He begged Brooke to prevent this:

> ... for fear of his interference with our people and Government there. If he would confine himself to the purposes of trade, of buying and selling, it would be of no consequence, but if he wishes to see *bichara*, to counsel or intrigue, or to exercise authority over our people, we beg of our friend to prevent him.

He added that Burns had bought some beads from Nakhodah Jelludeen, having agreed to pay for them on his return from Singapore with Ballachu cloth, but that Burns had failed to complete the bargain. The beads remained in Burns's possession, as the Nakhodah refused to take them back.

Robbie then planned to trade in Bintulu, but no one would give him passage and when he heard that a steamer was about to return with Brooke to Sarawak, he requested, politely and with due deference, to take passage as far as Bintulu.[4]

> Sometime ago, as your Excellency is aware, I visited several of the rivers along the coast to the westward of Bruni; amongst the number, I ascended the river Bintulu, and thence reached the country of the Kayans. During my stay amongst this little-known, independent, and powerful people, I had ample experience of their good faith and hospitality to warrant my stating that they are a people peaceably inclined, and in every respect favourably disposed for trade and friendly intercourse with Europeans. In a rough manner I have already endeavoured to lay before the public some account of them and their country; but my observations regarding a people so interesting being far from complete, I have determined on returning, and

intend penetrating further into the interior of the country, in order to ascertain correctly of its productions, and to make myself more familiar with the language and customs of the people. With this object in view, I have been now two months waiting at Labuan in expectation of an opportunity of getting to Bintulu, but unfortunately all my endeavours to procure a passage by any of the native vessels going to that place have been unsuccessful, on account, as I am led to believe, that a letter was sent from Sarawak to the Orang Kayas of Bintulu, instructing them not to open the Antimony Mines, nor allow any European to do so, nor yet reside at the place; and that in case of disobedience, a steamer would be sent from Sarawak to inflict summary punishment upon them. Whether from the same cause or not, I cannot tell, but the Nakhoda of a large Prahu that left this port for Bintulu, about twelve days ago, and to whom I applied for a passage, told me that he could not comply with my request, being in dread of your Excellency's displeasure.

Under these unfavourable circumstances, and as your Excellency purposes to return shortly to Sarawak by the steamer *Nemesis*, I respectfully request and hope that your Excellency will be pleased to permit my being landed at Bintulu by the steamer, on her way down the coast this time; my only plea for requesting this favour of your Excellency, and at the public cost, is, that although I am not paid for any bodily risk or expense I may incur in gratifying my inclination for travel in exploring any part of a comparatively unknown country, still, in my opinion, the same advantages will accrue as if I were employed by the public to do so.

I have the honour to be, Sir,
Your Excellency's very obedient servant,

ROBERT BURNS

Brooke[5] replied through Charles Grant on the same day:

Sir,

I am instructed by Sir James Brooke to inform you, that after your highly improper letter, he declines all further communication.

I have the honour to be, Sir,
Your obedient servant,

C. GRANT

Robbie[6] again wrote to Brooke on 19 June:

Feeling myself much aggrieved in consequence of a report, current both at this place and also at Singapore, stating that I was forcibly obliged to leave Bintulu by your Excellency's command, as a British subject, I take the liberty of requesting the necessary information on a matter of so great importance to myself and others, viz., whether British subjects have the privilege of trading with and of settling at any of the ports on the coast of Borneo, situated between Bruné and Sambas?

Brooke's[7] response was swift and curt:

Sir,

I am instructed by Sir James Brooke to refer you to Article II of the Treaty with the Sultan of Borneo, of which I enclose a copy for your information.

I am, &c.

C. GRANT

Burns remained in Borneo but before long, complaints about his conduct began to circulate. The great Kayan chief, Kum Nipa, according to Brooke[8], stated that Burns had let it be widely known that he was Brooke's son and that another chief, Kum Lassa, had been induced to give the young man his daughter in marriage. This snippet of gossip eventually reached Scotland where it appeared in the *Glasgow Courier* on 23 May 1850. 'Heaven bless me if I had such a son, or such a relative' wrote Brooke in his journal.

The *Straits Times* reported on 20 November 1849 that Burns was still on Labuan eager to return to his adoptive brothers, the Rejang Kayan. 'But the Malays continued, for some hidden reason, to refuse him passage', until Mr Napier, the Lieutenant-Governor used his authority and twice procured a perahu. However, even the elements were against him and on both occasions, Burns was compelled to return by strong contrary winds. On 22 January 1850, Burns landed in Singapore from Labuan on board the *Polka*,[9] a British schooner of 145 tons and he left again on the *Royalist* on 30 March 1850.[10]

Brooke[11] wrote to Burns from Singapore on 28 July 1850, informing him that the Sultan had requested Brooke to adjudicate on a case pending between Jelludeen and Burns relative to the sale of some beads. He reminded Burns that after a previous application in 1848, he had advised Burns, through Low, to settle such a trifling matter in private. But he also indicated that Burns had the option of leaving the decision to the government of Bruné, to Brooke or to any three arbitrators properly chosen and approved by Brooke. The Governor also regretted that the case had not been concluded and he requested Burns to settle in any of the three modes:

> I need only allude to the serious consequences which may result, should you longer refuse compliance with a very proper and very reasonable demand ...

Five months later, on Christmas Eve 1850, Brooke[12] awarded the sum of twenty-four dollars to Nakodah Jelludeen due to him by Robert Burns, supercargo in charge of the cutter *Young Frederick*.

> And the said Robert Burns having for two years past refused to settle this claim, or to refer it to my decision as Commissioner and Consul-General or to decide it by arbitration, I now call upon Robert Burns to submit peaceably to this award ...

Brooke's judgement ended with a call for all British subjects to assist in its execution and he gave the Sultan's government power to enforce it in Bruné.

Next day, Christmas 1850, Brooke sent Palmerston translations of replies sent to him by the Kinneah and Kayan Rajahs of Barram[13] in response to letters addressed to them by Brooke in January of that year 'seeking the establishment of friendly relations and the promotion of commerce'. He also requested that they 'desist from making hostile incursions into the territory of the Sultan of Bruné'. The copy of a third letter related to Burns's conduct:

> ... the first Englishman who has ever visited this interesting and important river. The statements set forth are more than confirmed by the testimony of David Cowan, the master of the small cutter in which he sailed, who declared that Mr Burns would have been put to death had it not been for the consideration of these chiefs towards the English.

The letter from the Rajahs of Barram[14] was addressed to Mr Scott and Mr Low, who govern the country of Labuan, &c.

> This [letter] is in place of a personal conference with our friends, and [by it] we wish to inform our friends the story of Mr Burns having entered the country of Barram. We were under the impression that the reason of his wishing to visit us was to attend to his trade and business, and to deal with us truly in all affairs. We [on our parts] were very anxious to trade after the manner usual amongst merchants; but this, we inform our friends, Mr Scott and Mr Low, that Mr Burns does very treacherously (baniak rachow); he wishes (andak) to take persons' wives: whether they like it or not, he takes people's wives. And also Mr Burns ordered us to kill (potong) people who enter the River Barram, of whatsoever description (or race) they be; whoever enters it is good to kill them, saying (Mr Burns) 'whatever you want, Tama – itam – Balari, I will give you; muskets, ten cases with powder and ball; and should it ever be inquired into at any future day, I will be responsible for all.
>
> Further, Nakodah Gadore tells us to take the whole matter to Labuan, and make it known to Mr Scott and Mr Low, but Mr Burns dissuaded us, saying he himself would bring the matter before the Court.

Brooke's letter to Palmerston continued:

The conduct of Mr Burns has been the same in every place which he
has visited, and there are numerous complaints against him ...

He enclosed a copy of his reply to the chiefs:

I request that in future, whenever an Englishman does wrong like Mr
Burns, my friends will order him out of their country, and hold no
intercourse with him, and should he refuse obedience, or otherwise
commit crime, or conduct himself badly, my friends can act justly
and rightly in support of their authority, and for the protection of
their people ... I trust in the friendship and fairness of the Rajahs of
Barram in dealing with white men; but white men cannot be permitted to behave like Mr Burns, or to commit crimes, or to cheat, or to
trade unfairly ... My friends must remember that no trader has any
authority to speak upon subjects concerning the Government of the
country, or to intrigue, or to spread false reports. Let the traders,
therefore, in my friends' country, be confined to their own business;
and if they represent themselves to be great people, possessed of
power, or talk as Mr Burns talked, my friends will know that they
speak falsely, and are men without shame.

This letter ended with the usual courtesies and was accompanied by a
gift of red cloth.

Brooke also sent Palmerston copies of two letters from Burns relating
to 'a trifling case' of the sale of beads, which had been pending between
him and Nakodah Jalludeen of Bruné, since 1847. Brooke stated that in the
absence of a reply to his first letter to Burns and Burns's previous refusal
to submit the case to decision, Brooke tried it in his absence and recommended that the Sultan enforce payment of twenty-four dollars anytime
Burns was in his territory.

Chapter XI

Maludu Bay

Robbie returned to Singapore on 10 May 1851 from 'Malluda, Labuan and the coast of Borneo' on board a cutter, the *Young Frederick*.[1] He was accompanied by Paker Mahomed, a native of Bombay, whom he had met in Maludu. Mahomed had been Chota Tindal (Bo'sun's mate) aboard the *Sultana*, a ship of 700 tons that was lost in the South China Sea more than ten years earlier. The *Sultana* was loaded with cotton when she was struck by lightning on 4 January 1841. Her Master, Captain Page, had scarcely ordered her three boats to be hoisted out before flames erupted fore and aft. The fury of the blaze was such that there was no time to secure provisions in the cutter and the jolly-boat which were lashed together. The rope parted on the fifth day and the cutter, with forty-one survivors that included the Captain, his pregnant wife and two female passengers, eventually reached Labuan, subsisting on daily rations of half a ship's biscuit and one cup of water. They then crossed to Brunei to seek help in returning to Singapore, but they were stripped of their few possessions and held for almost nine months in virtual captivity, until the intervention of James Brooke and the Honourable Company's steamer, *Diana*.

Mahomed and his companions were less fortunate; their craft drifted at the whim of wind and tide until on the tenth day they were cast ashore on the Bornean coast, about two days' sail from Maludu. Found by a fisherman, they were taken before the local headman, Sheriff Usman, who kept three prisoners for himself and sold the rest into slavery. Robbie was moved by Mahomed's account and offered him passage to Singapore, where he took him to Mr Church, the Resident Councillor. Mahomed was not prevented from leaving Maludu nor was he treated as a slave, presumably because he was 'employed' as a priest during captivity and taught the Koran to the children of a Pangeran.

Robbie remained in Singapore and on 28 June 1851 he wrote[2] belatedly to Lord Palmerston complaining of the 'obstructions and discouragements' that he had received in 'the prosecution of my lawful and authorized views in that interesting and little-known region'. He also recalled an application made to the Foreign Office in 1848, to sanction a negotiation which he 'had entered into with the Sultan of Borneo Proper, on behalf of a highly respectable mercantile firm of this island and Glasgow [Hamilton, Gray] to work the antimony mines in Bintulu and other adjoining districts under my immediate superintendence on the spot.' In furtherance of this object he travelled to Bintulu in February 1848 with an escort provided by the Sultan of Brunei and bearing a letter to the native chiefs of the country.

Robbie stated that he had lived in the Bintulu region for about a month when an armed perahu arrived from Sarawak, dispatched by Brooke's representative or deputy in the government of that territory, with a letter to the Bintulu chiefs 'in which they were informed that they were not to permit any white man either to work the mines or to reside in the country; and that if they disobeyed, a steamer would be sent up from Sarawak to punish them.' The letter was read out in Robbie's presence to the Bintulu chiefs, the Pangerans, who accompanied him from Brunei and in the hearing of several hundred natives. It bore the seal of the Sarawak Government and was signed by A. Crookshank for Raja Brooke.

Robbie asked the Bintulu chiefs if they were subject to Sarawak or if they would respect the authority of the Sultan of Brunei and he 'was not interfered with'. He added that had he 'not been resident long enough among them to ingratiate himself with the chiefs and people, and bearing the letter of the Sultan', the consequences might have been serious and have affected his personal safety. Crookshank's letter was subsequently conveyed to Brunei and Burns learned that it was delivered to the Sultan or to one of his ministers.

Robbie took care not to imply that Brooke was accountable for this act which was done during the latter's visit to England, but he maintained that the interference of Brooke's representative in Sarawak 'with the undoubted rights and privileges alike of British subjects and natives of Borneo, and such an assumption of Sarawak superiority to be upheld by British armed force over the Bintulu chiefs, called for due consideration at the hands of Her Majesty's Commissioner in Borneo.'

Robbie then sought Palmerston's opinion on correspondence which he had enclosed and asked if his representations on the subject were deemed so improper that Brooke declined to have any further communication with him (Burns). He wrote that:

I cannot pretend to any acquaintance with official forms of correspondence, and I can only say that I did not mean to be disrespectful in stating that I believed that it was in consequence of the interference from Sarawak above referred to, and of their dread of the supposed displeasures of his Excellency, should they convey me to the coast, that the natives declined giving me a passage.

Robbie protested that his letter did not deserve the decisive and summary rebuff which his application received and he submitted that Brooke must be considered as 'adopting the responsibility of an unjustifiable interference with the intercourse of British subjects with the natives of Borneo for lawful objects.' Robbie cited a similar example of Brooke's policy in afterwards addressing a letter to the Chiefs of Bintulu, calling upon them to turn him out of the country. The letter was delivered by the Honourable Company's steamer, *Phlegethon* from Singapore, shortly after Brooke's arrival from England. Burns received it in Bintulu in July 1848, soon after his return from Kayan country. Like the first letter, it was read before the Chiefs in Burns's presence and in the hearing of a large audience of natives. But the letter did not inconvenience Robbie and did not prevent several of the principal Chiefs and a large body of natives from accompanying him aboard the steamer to the mouth of the river.

Robbie also complained that Brooke used 'his influence to excite hostile feelings towards me among the natives, and to spread, both amongst them and among Europeans, derogatory views of my character and objects.'

In his defence, Burns wrote of the welcome that he was always given by the natives, their regret at parting with him, the perfect fearlessness with which he entrusted himself among them, wholly unaccompanied.

The humble state in which Sir James Brooke found me seeking to visit them, alone and unattended in a native trading Prahu when he refused me a passage in the steamer *Nemesis*, constitutes a sufficient answer to such misrepresentations.

During the voyage to which Robbie alluded, he was a witness of the overbearing conduct of the Prahus from Sarawak 'toward the ignorant and defenceless natives' and he cited other examples.

Burns claimed that the Treaty between Her Majesty, Queen Victoria and the Sultan of Brunei was wholly unknown or completely misunderstood on the coast during his recent voyage and that:

> This circumstance has induced me to get a number of copies in the Malay language lithographed at the place, with the intention of distributing them in the various rivers which I mean to visit in the course of another voyage, on which I hope to start in the course of a few days more, and in which my trading occupations will facilitate the acquisition of information regarding the country, so desirable for many reasons.
>
> Before concluding, I hope your Lordship will allow me to observe that, although the circumstance of my objects being exclusively mercantile might alone justify me in laying my case before your Lordship, yet I may further urge that my residence among aboriginal races of the North-west Coast hitherto unvisited by Europeans, had been the means of bringing before the public the first authentic, though scanty information, regarding them.

Robbie appended the editor's comments on his first paper published in February 1849.

The letter subsequently appeared in the London *Examiner* on 4 October, 1851 and in *The North British Daily Mail*, two days later.[3] The Glasgow newspaper also printed Burns's correspondence with Brooke, in which he requested transport to Bintulu aboard the *Nemesis* on the Raja's return to Sarawak.

'ROBERT BURNS' AND SIR JAMES BROOKE.

We cannot decline to publish the subjoined letters. They relate a somewhat curious transaction, to which the parties are Sir James Brooke, Rajah of Sarawak, and Mr Robert Burns, namesake and grandson of the great poet, now seeking his fortune among the 'slaves spicy forests and gold-bubbling fountains' of Borneo. Sir James Brooke, her Majesty's Commissioner, her Majesty's Consul-General, and her Majesty's Governor of the Free Port of Labuan, exercises, as is well known, a monopoly of the antimony mines of Sarawak. These mines were supposed to be the richest in the world, until Mr Burns found mines equally rich in the territory of the independent Sultan of Borneo, 150 miles away from the territory of Rajah Brooke. On the latter discovery, Mr Burns obtained permission from the native prince to work the mines; but it would seem that the dignitary who is paid from the British Exchequer to insure fair play to British industry can 'bear no brother near his throne,' and has not scrupled to employ the power of the Crown to obstruct fair competition. It is an ugly-looking affair, and ought to be sifted. Of Mr Burns, all we know is that he is an adventurous traveller; that he has mastered two of the languages of Borneo; that he has penetrated farther into that great and little-known island than any other European; that he has written by far the best and most authentic account of it (in the 'Journal of the Archipelago') that has ever been given to the public; and that over and above such claims he is of a name and race that should at least entitle him to consideration and respect wherever civilized men abide. The grand-daughter of Milton had the sympathies of our grandsires in the last century; and justice ought not to be denied to the grandson of Robert Burns in the present. Sir James Brooke is the hero and principal author of four octavo volumes, and of innumerable fugitive puffs. He has some claim, therefore, to be considered as one of 'the craft'. Yet to judge by his treatment of the son of an editor of the 'Edinburgh Review', and of the grandson of a great poet, he would not appear to be imbued with much reverence for letters.

On 7 October, the paper[4] thundered its censure against Brooke.

The letters which we published yesterday from 'Mr Robert Burns,' grandson of the Bard, to Lord Palmerston, exhibit Sir James Brooke and his government of Sarawak in a very unfavourable light. The knotty point in the recent controversy concerning the Rajah was, whether the Dyaks slain by his Excellency's commands were pirates or not pirates? If pirates, the law would justify the massacre of Borneo, whatever humanity might say of it. If not pirates, it was all over with Sir James Brooke, morally and legally. But this point has never been satisfactorily settled, each party maintaining its own view with unyielding pertinacity. There can be no such difficulty, however, in the present case. To mistake the grandson of Robert Burns for a Bintulu pirate is too gross and unaccountable a blunder even for a Rajah Brooke to make with impunity. The impression left by the documents in our columns yesterday is, that Mr Burns has been most harshly and unjustly treated by Sir James Brooke and that a system of tyranny is established in the Indian Archipelago, essentially hostile to enterprise, to commerce and to civilisation.

Why should not Mr Burns be as free to explore, to open mines and to establish trading relations in the Archipelago as Sir James Brooke?' What was Sir James himself but a poor friendless adventurer when he began his career in the Indian Seas? Is Borneo to be less accessible to the enterprise of British subjects since, than it was before, the elevation of Rajah Brooke over Sarawak? As long as Mr Burns does not poach on Sir James Brooke's manor, we do not see why the latter should be suffered to interfere with him; and the country which condemned the Scottish Bard to a guagership [sic], would be utterly inexcusable if it closed the path of honourable adventure to his grandson.

What are the facts of the case? Mr Burns has been travelling for some years in the island of Borneo. He has penetrated farther into the interior of that little-known region than any other European. He has mastered two of the languages of the country, and has published an account of the manners and customs of the people, which is admitted by competent judges to be the best work on the subject. In the course of his travels, Mr Burns discovered some very rich antimony mines in Bintulu; and in connection with a mercantile firm in Glasgow, proposed to work them, with permission of the native prince. Negotiations were opened by him for this purpose, which, so far as they had gone, appear to have been quite successful. Mr Burns, possessing probably some of the cordial qualities of his grandfather, soon ingratiated himself into the favour of the Sultan and the native chiefs. Bintulu forms no part of the territory over which Sir James Brooke is Rajah. Mr Burns was thus breaking up new ground, and bringing new territories under the dominion of British commerce. But this was precisely the circumstance which seems to have rendered his proceedings disagreeable to Rajah Brooke; for his Excellency is proprietor of the antimony mines of

Sarawak, and to allow an independent company to work the antimony mines of Bintulu, would have been to destroy his own monopoly. The whole influence of the Rajah, therefore, was exerted to disparage Mr Burns in the estimation of the native chiefs, to dissuade and intimidate them from forming any engagements with him — in short, to ruin his project and drive him out of the country. We might here ask by what authority Sir James Brooke could act in this manner? He is 'her Majesty's Commissioner and Consul-General to the Independent Princes of Borneo'; but it is not the usual practice of the Queen herself, still less of her consuls, to assert a commercial monopoly over the territories to which they are commissioned; and it would have been more consistent with the nature of Sir James Brooke's office to have facilitated than obstructed such relations as Mr Burns was forming with the native princes. So effectual were the efforts of the Rajah and his agents to alarm and intimidate the natives, that Mr Burns could not obtain a passage in any of their vessels from Labuan to Bintulu; and on praying his Excellency to allow him to go on board the steamer *Nemesis*, the great man informed him, through his secretary, that he declined to have any further communication with him.

The unsophisticated Robert Burns, little used, like his great progenitor, to the honeyed phrase of courtiers, was quite astounded by this rebuff; and 'in venturing to address' Lord Palmerston, he manifests a certain tremor like a man walking over a volcano, and hopes and trusts that he has expressed himself 'in a manner sufficiently respectful and becoming.' We venture to believe that our young countryman will find Lord Palmerston much less punctilious than his lofty Excellency of Sarawak, and that his complaints, honestly and boldly stated, will now receive a deliberate and impartial consideration.

This affair of Mr Burns throws a sinister light on the massacre of the Dyaks. By a series of relentless butcheries, the Rajah of Sarawak succeeds in striking terror into the natives of Borneo, and this terror is employed by his Excellency to defeat such laudable enterprises as that of Mr Burns, and to rivet his own monopoly. British arms are thus employed to destroy British industry.

We begin to have serious misgivings regarding Rajah Brooke.

Establishing himself in Sarawak as a trader, and acquiring great influence over the natives, his achievements were hailed in this country with extraordinary favour; he was hero-worshipped by the people; applauded by the press; knighted and Rajah-ed by the Queen; and, like many favourites of fortune before him, we fear that so many honours have turned his head. His conduct towards Mr Burns is that of a man who cannot bear a rival near his throne; and he would evidently prefer Borneo to remain a savage waste than to pour its riches into any other hands than his own. It is necessary that the Government should institute the most rigid inquiry into the whole proceedings of Sir James Brooke; and, whatever be the result, of this fact Lord Palmerston and his colleagues may rest fully assured – that monopoly, driven out of this country, shall not be permitted to take refuge, under any pretence, in the Indian Archipelago.

Seven weeks after mailing his letter to Palmerston, Burns set sail on his last trading venture, determined to visit the north-east coast of Borneo and to ascend the Kinabatangan River, which he learned was rich in camphor and edible birds' nests. A further inducement may have been added in Labuan, his first port of call. There in August:

> ... some boats from Kini Batangnan on the East Coast of Borneo brought valuable cargoes of bird's nests, camphor and elephant's tusks of a large size, a pair of the heaviest weighing above 50 catties. ... The Nakodahs who trade to the East Coast of Borneo are said to be unanimous in their testimony regarding elephants being numerous in the neighbourhood of Kini Batangnan. They say that these animals frequently approach within a short distance of the houses but are seldom mischievous.

The report continued that the names Kini Balu, Kini Batagnan suggest the existence of Chinese settlements 'in ancient times' and that the elephants 'may be descended from animals imported' from Asia.[5]

Robbie was aboard the *Dolphin*, owned by Walter Scott Paterson of Singapore and listed in the Singapore press under 'Native Craft, British'. She was a schooner of 60 tons that wore the British flag and her skipper was a Captain Robertson of Leith. The *Dolphin* had spent several months in harbour before making for Labuan and Brunei on 19 July 1851.[6]

The schooner rounded the most northerly cape of Borneo in early September and entered Maludu Bay where Robbie arranged for the chief of the main village to pilot the schooner to the Kinabatangan, but the *Dolphin* ran aground. Robbie was incandescent with rage and upbraided the Captain. They exchanged blows and Burns, who sustained a black eye, had his hands tied behind him. Robbie and the boat were eventually freed, but Robertson refused to continue and it was agreed that they would return to Labuan. However, disaster struck before the *Dolphin* turned about.

Several writers have cited this incident in support of Robbie's alleged aggressive and intemperate behaviour, but in a subsequent deposition, the Kasab (storesman) of the *Dolphin* stated that 'The Captain and Mr Burns were good friends generally, but at Maludu, they had words about the vessel's getting aground.[7]

Chapter XII

The Amok

The Sulu archipelago, which is now part of the Southern Philippines, consists of a double chain of volcanic and coral islands that lies between Mindanao and the eastern shores of Sabah, formerly British North Borneo. This archipelago, like the rest of the Philippines, was largely populated by successive migrations from South-East Asia mainly by way of Borneo. Islam followed routes pioneered by Indian and Arab traders and by the mid-fifteenth century it had dominated the Sulu islands and the coast of Mindanao. These fiercely independent peoples lived by the sea as fishermen, traders and dealers in slaves, but the most notorious and feared were the Illanun (Lanun) who originated from Mindanao and settled the Sulus before inhabiting the islands and coasts of North Borneo. The Illanun often formed communities with the Bajaus, and with the Balagnini tribe in particular, who dwelt on a cluster of small islands near Sulu.

Hugh Low[1] described how in the 1840s:

> ... the coast is annually infested by the fleets from the Soolu Archipelago, which, leaving their own islands situated on the N.E. of Borneo, about the middle of the N.E. monsoon, sail round the island with a fair wind stretching across to the coasts of Java, Banca Singapore, and the peninsula, and visiting all the islands in the way ...

These pirates were ruthless; burning, destroying, killing, looting, and selling those they spared into slavery. The Illanuns usually cruised in small squadrons of up to seventy sail, but on occasion, two hundred boats might run before the wind through the South China Sea. The Balagnini behaved in a similar fashion, but favoured the waters of Brunei whose inhabitants were essentially peace-loving and ready quarry. The annual depredations so terrified the populace that the northeasterly wind that brought the raiders was known as the Pirate Wind.

On 2 December 1851, the following item appeared in the *Straits Times*:[2]

It is our melancholy duty to record a fearful outrage committed by a party of Lanun and Suloo pirates – the sea rovers of the Archipelago whose atrocities have been overlooked or winked at by our naval authorities – on the north east coast of Borneo. Had our ships of war, during the past ten years, been employed in driving from these and the neighbouring seas the formidable Lanun, Suloo and Magindanzo pirates, instead of aiding in the intertribal wars of the tribes of the Sarawak, Sadong and Sakarran rivers, PIRACY would long since have been put down, and such a tragedy as it is now our painful duty to narrate would not have taken place.

The atrocity was then described by an unnamed correspondent and his account was largely substantiated by another 'independent, but reliable source at Labuan ... ' One week later, the paper published the depositions of the surviving members of the crew and those first obtained by St John,[3] the Acting Commissioner at Labuan, form the basis of the summary that follows.

The *Dolphin* left the Maludu river after the row between Burns and the captain. Kreemon, the Serang (Bo'sun), listed the complement: Captain Robertson, the supercargo Burns, ten lascars (seamen) all Javanese, three jurumudies (coxswains) and himself. He did not include the captain's nona (woman) who was below deck. The press reports were uncertain of the precise date of the attack, but the Serang stated that it was on the fourteenth day of the Arabic month of Dulkaida, which corresponded to the 10 September. The schooner had left the river mouth and at about noon, two perahu were seen heading in its direction, they resembled large sampans but were broader in the beam than local craft. When within hailing distance, the crews called that they wished to trade and they asked for fish and rice. There were ten men and a boy in the two vessels which came alongside and six men armed with sundangs boarded the *Dolphin*, saying they wished to trade. Burns said, 'Stop till we anchor.' The visitors then brought 'musters of Tortoiseshell and Pearls' but no business was transacted that day and they returned to their boats which held astern during the night.

At about seven o'clock the following morning, eight or nine men came aboard armed as before and suddenly Captain Robertson ran for'ard, bleeding from a face wound. At that time the crew was in the bows replacing the flying jib-boom and the Serang believed that no one saw the start of the amok. Robertson ran out on the boom crying, 'Jangan lawan, jangan lawan, lari!' (Don't fight, don't fight, run!) Three or four pirates armed with sundangs and spears were in pursuit and the captain was never seen again. One crewman heard the skipper plead for his life and those of his men, before Robertson fell into the sea and sank. The raiders then turned on the crew, butchering one jurumudi on deck and cutting down a boy, Burns's servant, near the foremast. The survivors jumped into the sea where one lascar was speared to death from a perahu.

There were no witnesses to the killings as the crew was for'ard, but one of the *Straits Times's* correspondents[4] stated that:

> Whilst Mr Burns was in a stooping posture his attention taken up examining some pearls in his hand, a Borneo mat, rolled up, was handed from that boat, which Burns glanced at, and in which was concealed a Suloo kris; the pretended trader adroitly drew out the hidden weapon, and at a single cut severed Burns' head from his body. Captain Robertson was pacing up and down the quarterdeck, and at this juncture his back was towards Burns. The Suloo man, observing Burns despatched, made a cut at Robertson's neck ...

The carnage ceased when a pirate called, 'Do you wish to live or die? If you wish to live come on board and lift the anchor.' On this the crew returned to the *Dolphin* where their hands were tied and each was asked, 'Will you sail the ship and live or refuse and die?' The pirates held their swords aloft as each seaman answered, 'We wish to live.' The schooner weighed anchor and made for open water with Burns's corpse hard by the wheel and the pirates said, 'Let the vessel get out to sea a little before we throw the bodies overboard.'

According to this report Burns had one wound across the forehead, one on the neck and one on the side; he was covered in blood. The Serang thought that he must have been struck from behind as all the wounds were on the right side; the body was thrown into the sea. Burns's servant 'was very much wounded in five or six places' and the nona, who had been found below, had one large wound on the side of her neck and they, with the dead coxswain, were consigned to the depths. The rumour of Burns's death and the seizure of his boat that had circulated in Labuan eight months earlier[5] was now sadly confirmed.

Commenting on the depositions in its issue of 9 December, the *Straits Times* observed that:

> These statements leave us totally in the dark as to the commence-ment of the attack, the crew manifesting neither curiosity or alarm on the alleged traders boarding the vessel at Malludu; not one was an eye-witness of the wounds inflicted on Mr Burns or captain Robertson, and their first intimation of the Massacre which was going on was the captain's endeavouring to reach the jib-boom after having been wounded, and upon seeing which the crew, in the utmost consternation, jumped overboard.

All the arms were meanwhile stowed safely below deck.

In their depositions the survivors implicated Sheriff Hossain, the Chief of Maludu, in the murders, noting that on the night before the attack there were two perahu, while in the morning there were three. Hossain was in the third boat.

Having disposed of the dead, the Lanuns made for Benggaya in Labuk Bay which they reached nine days later, stopping in the mouth of the river to fire a seven-gun salute. Immediately a boat from Sheriff Yasin, the local Rajah, came alongside and demanded, 'Whose vessel is this?'

'It is mine' cried Memadam the leader of the pirates.

The Rajah's men insisted that the vessel belonged to Mr Burns. Memadam denied this saying, 'It belongs to another European.'

The Rajah's boat then pulled for the shore.

Next morning, three pirates and six survivors left the *Dolphin* and stayed on shore for two days; then twenty-four of the Rajah's men went out to the schooner. The original crew were told, 'Keep aloof, we are sent to take the vessel from the Lanuns; if they do not give it up we will kill them, so keep clear of the affray.'

The Lanuns obeyed the Rajah's order and were taken ashore where two of their number lay dead; their faces were unmarked but their bodies 'were chopped and hacked almost to pieces.' The Rajah told the Serang and two of his shipmates to take their heads as he was anxious to send them to Labuan.

'These men were murderers: take their heads and preserve them in salt and sopee, gin or arrack, as an evidence that I have assisted the

Europeans.'

Memadam, the pirate leader escaped into the jungle with two surviving lascars who probably fled, fearful of the circumstances. The remaining Lanuns were held for some time, pending the arrival of a steamer from Labuan, but the Rajahs from Sulu thrice demanded that they should be given up and they were; the Lanun chiefs were aboard their boats in considerable force in a nearby river and the local Rajah was greatly outnumbered.

Later it was reported that a steamer was in the vicinity so the Serang from the *Dolphin* went in a small boat and told the story 'to a gentleman belonging to Rajah Brooke'. This was St John, Brooke's Acting Commissioner, who ordered the heads to be thrown overboard. On 25 November 1851, St John, now in Labuan, wrote to the naval Commander-in-Chief, Rear-Admiral Charles Austen and recounted the fate of the *Dolphin*. By that time the schooner was on passage to Singapore in charge of an officer from *Pluto* and manned by four ratings and the survivors of the amok. They reached port on 1 December where statements were sworn before the Honourable Thomas Church, the Resident Councillor.

When the pirates took the *Dolphin,* they ransacked the boat and threw nearly all the books, clothes and papers over the side. Some property was also landed at Maludu but Burns's journal was overlooked and was later found when the schooner was back in British hands. In one of his last entries, Burns[6] complained of ill-treatment by Captain Robertson in consequence of a misunderstanding between them about the delivery of some cargo sold to the Imam, 'and soliciting the interference of Sherif Hossain'. The entry for 27 August read:

> I requested the Imam to send to Malluda for the Orang Besar [the headman] in order that I might not be abused further.

It appeared that some people from the village boarded the *Dolphin* and that Burns was released upon their arrival. On 31 August, the diary read, 'evening, Sherif Hossain came from Malluda' and on 4 September, Burns wrote, 'about 7 a.m., I started for Malluda to collect small debts, etc. and returned by sunset.'

Burns penned his final entry on Saturday, 6 September 1851.

Sherif Hossain arrived early this morning from Tabour and said a steamer was outside yesterday an [sic] anchor off Tanjong Sampong.

The *Straits Times* thought that it was a Spanish vessel 'unless Sherif Hossain desired to deceive Burns.' It continued:

... from the foregoing it would appear clear that Sherif Hossain was almost daily on board the schooner, and knew what was going on: taking these circumstances and the statements on oath of the *Dolphin's* against Sherif Hossain, and one which ought to be taken up by the British authorities.

Eleven years later, St John recounted the fate of the *Dolphin* in *Life in the Forests of the Far East*[7] stating that he had been provided with the steamer, *Pluto*, to gain first-hand information on the pirate communities of the northeast coast of Borneo.

The ship had just anchored in Maludu Bay when Sheriff Hasan came with news of the murders. The following morning, St John set off at first light in an armed cutter for Maludu town and 'after three hours' pull we arrived, poling our way up the narrow creek to the houses.' There he spoke with the headmen, including Sheriff Hossain, who was aboard the *Dolphin* while Burns was negotiating with the Lanuns and Sulus. Hossain said that he was looking over the stern talking to men in his perahu when he turned and 'saw Burns fall before the kris of a Sulu and the Lanun cutting at the English captain.' Hossain was not molested because of his 'sacred character' and he hurried ashore in his boat.

Leaving Maludu, *Pluto* steamed along the coast amid the shoals, reaching Benggaya, the home of Sheriff Yasin, but the river could not be found. However, next morning, two canoes approached from shore with survivors from the *Dolphin* and a messenger from Yasin. St John was informed that the schooner was safe upstream and that her cargo, on board and in the village, was untouched. St John embarked in a ship's boat and after pulling upriver for fifteen miles, they found the *Dolphin* guarded by Yasin's men, with the hatches nailed and the cabin door secured. The deck was still stained with blood which was also spattered on the white paint of the cabin.

St John learned that Yasin's village was a further fifteen miles upstream, so he and a friend transferred to a light native canoe and with a strong crew pulling hard they reached their goal about half-past nine on a clear, moonlit night. Next morning, St John was up at daybreak taking depositions when he noticed a number of Sulus leaning over twenty-five barrels of gunpowder smoking cigars. Yasin then showed him part of the schooner's cargo which he had stowed in his inner room; this consisted of arms, guns, powder, cloth and a number of small articles. 'After a good breakfast, and a friendly parting' St John set off downstream, covering around fifteen miles in three hours on a fast ebb. When they reached the *Dolphin* they were met by the *Pluto's* boats, sent by an anxious captain fearful of St John's safety. The *Dolphin* was got under weigh and joined *Pluto* after a long hard day. The following morning the schooner was readied for sea and towed part way to Labuan en route to Singapore.

Years later, in his biography of Brooke published in 1879, St John[8] wrote that he discovered among Burns's papers on the *Dolphin*:

> ... not only proofs of their [Hume and Burns] having endeavoured to bribe the Sultan to complain of Sir James Brooke, but I found a very curious argument written out, whether it would not be justifiable on his [Mr Burns's] part to receive slaves in payment of goods. His conclusion was that he would be completely justified. And this is a specimen of the men who banded against Sir James Brooke.

Chapter XIII

The *Dolphin* Avenged

St John's dispatch to Admiral Austen in November 1851 was forwarded to Captain T. L. Massie RN, Senior Officer in the Straits of
Malacca. In an acknowledgment to the Hon T. Church, Resident
Councillor in Singapore, Massie not only deplored the killings at Maludu
but remarked that it was curious that although St John was 'on the spot, and
taken the several depositions, he does not in any way allude to Sheriff
Hossain, as connected with the above treacherous attack.'[1] This Maludu
chief had been implicated in the murders by the *Dolphin*'s crew.

The Governor of Prince of Wales' Island, Singapore and Malacca, the
Honourable E. A. Blundell, wrote to Massie on 22 December,[2] stating that
he had again looked over the depositions which he now returned.

I am at a loss to comprehend Mr St John's proceedings. He goes to
the N.E. Coast, purposely to examine into the affair of the *Dolphin*,
yet he seems to put it aside as a secondary matter, and sends the
Admiral a number of depositions to the effect, that a place called
Tunku is a resort of Pirates. He is at Malludu and hears from Sheriff
Houssain himself that he was not present on board the *Dolphin*,
when she was taken, yet he never questions that personage as to his
doings on board, or examines any of the crew on that point. Neither
does he bring to the Admiral's notice the fact, of this man being on
board, when the murders were committed. Sheriff Yasin is very
highly praised by him, and it may be with perfect justice, but the
whole story of the recapture of the *Dolphin* wears a curious look and
the stories of the narrators, are very inconsistent with each other.
Sheriff Yasin, tells Mr St John, that he took the Schooner after a
sharp resistance, when two pirates were killed. The *Dolphin*'s crew
say these 2 men were put to death ashore and that when an armed
party came off, all (or nearly all) the pirates had gone ashore apparently to the Rajah, as Sheriff Yasin is called by them.

There is nothing in any of the depositions relating to the Cargo
on board when taken by the Pirates, and that on board, when the

vessel is given up to the *Pluto*. If intact, so much in favor of Sheriff Yasin. If otherwise it confirms the suspicion of collusion between Sheriff Yasin and the Pirates.

Memadam, the head Pirate goes ashore with 2 or 3 followers, flies into the jungle (when, is unknown) yet threatens to bring a force to retake the vessel. Sheriff Yasin, known to have but 70 fighting men, is allowed to keep possession, for 40 or 50 days, of a vessel with a valuable cargo, rescued from Pirates, who are said to swarm in the neighbourhood.

Mr St John makes no comment on these points taken from his depositions. He does not tell the Admiral, how he first obtained intelligence of the *Dolphin's* loss. By the way, he says, she was cut off in August, whereas the depositions taken by him on the 26th October and 1st November say, about 40 days before, nor does he state what relations have hitherto held between Sheriff Yasin, Sheriff Houssain, and Sarawak or Labuan.

Not having any Map of Borneo and its neighbourhood the positions of Tunku and other Pirate resorts are unknown to me.

There seems no doubt of Sheriff Houssain being implicated in the piracy, and I should say that Malludu is the place whence redress should be claimed, while against Tunku there is no evidence (in the *Dolphin's* case) except the belief that Memadam, the leading Pirate resides there. He may have changed his residence the now a dependent of Sheriff Houssain of Malludu.

The Commander-in-Chief, Admiral Austen, was on board HMS *Hastings* at Hong Kong at that time and Massie was obliged to await orders. They arrived in dispatches to the Secretary of the Admiralty and to Massie, written on 29 December 1851 and they reveal remarkable sensitivity and tact on the part of a senior officer, in a service notorious for its brutality on board its own ships. Perhaps this reflected Austen's background, he was a brother of Jane, but his delicacy of feeling could have well been enhanced by public hostility in Singapore and Britain towards the navy's role in the South China Sea.

Austen[3] 'desired' Massie to take any of the surviving *Dolphin's* crew and his squadron that consisted of HMS *Cleopatra* and the HC steamers, *Semiramis* and *Pluto*, to the place indicated in St John's communication, where he was to secure a safe anchorage. From there, the boats of *Cleopatra* and *Semiramis* were to ascend the Tungkee river covered by *Pluto*. The officer in command of the expedition was to prepare for sudden attack and presuming that they had not been met with in force on their way up the river, and that the expedition reached Tungkee without molestation, it would be:

> ... for the officer in charge to endeavour to ascertain whether the allegation of the Acting Commissioner [St John], that the pirates consisted of Lannus and Sulus, under the command of a Lannu from Tungkee is correct; further, whether the inhabitants of Tungkee consist, as is represented, of a community of pirates; and in this it is to be observed, that a nice question is involved, and that the strongest presumptive evidence of its being a pirate settlement would not of itself justify us in the destruction of the place ... I am myself of opinion that they will be met with in force on the river ...

Austen enjoined that the young chief, Sheriff Yassin, who recaptured the schooner and who reported the circumstances to Labuan, 'should not be suffered to be molested'. However, despite Austen's doubts that Yasin was beyond suspicion, he wished Massie to visit the chief and thank him on behalf of the British Government. The Commander-in-Chief concluded his dispatch by stating his 'utmost reliance' on Massie's judgement and discretion and to bear in mind:

> ... that while the tragic proceedings on board the *Dolphin* call for vengeance on the perpetrators of the acts, yet it is better that many guilty should escape, than one innocent man should suffer.

On 30 January 1852, *Cleopatra* arrived in the bay at Pulo Gaya and the following morning, with all his boats manned and armed, Captain Massie called on the Pangeran who was suspected of some involvement with the pirates. The British flag was saluted with twenty-one guns. The boats returned the courtesy and Massie began a conference of some length during which a 'lecture' was read to the Pangeran. The *Cleopatra* then made for Maludu Bay where Massie was anxious to find out if the community and Sheriff Hossain, in particular, were connected with the affair of the *Dolphin*. But on the night of their arrival 'deluges of rain' fell which continued unceasingly for the rest of the week; 'the freshes' made it utterly impossible to ascend the river. In the meantime, Sheriff Hossain visited Massie on board and he appeared to speak 'clearly and honestly' when bluntly accused of his alleged part in the murders. Hossain added, 'There is the best reason in the world I should not be concerned in such a business since the English have two of my brothers at Sarawak.' Massie remarked that the surviving crew of the *Dolphin* seldom told the same story twice and if they were posed a leading question they would answer exactly the way they are led. 'The lawyers must find the truth of all this at Singapore.'

Massie reported his attack on Tungku to the Commander-in-Chief on 19 February.[4] The river mouth had been hard to find but after securing an anchorage, he sent boats upstream bearing a flag of truce, a signal 'generally respected by the natives of the other coast.' But the boats came under fire from different parts of the jungle leaving one man dead and two dangerously wounded. Massie elected to destroy the settlement.

The shallow river mouth prevented *Pluto* from covering the assault, so the ships' boats crossed the bar at high tide and after dusk, where they remained at anchor until 2.30 a.m. This gave ample time to pull upriver in the cool of the morning and to reach the stockade about first light. The high river banks favoured surprise attacks by the pirates, so flanking parties of marines were landed on both sides; the stockade was taken at 5.30 a.m. and the jungle was cleared for several miles. As one Malay observed, 'The whole was reduced to charcoal.'

While the jungle was being cleared and the settlement torched, the 'invisible' enemy launched an unexpected attack on the boats, wounding three sailors from the *Cleopatra*, one fatally. The advance parties returned at around half-past twelve 'having revenged as far as possible the murder of Messrs. Burns and Robertson as well as the wanton and treacherous attack upon the flag of truce.'

Massie was surprised that his casualties were so light, given the ease with which the river banks could have been defended. Conditions were appalling, his shore parties marched knee-deep in leech-infested mud, opposed by almost impassable jungle, in hot, humid conditions, while the boats' crews sweltered under a burning sun in the heavy uniforms of the day, for twelve of the twenty-four hour operation.

Massie then thanked his officers and men, regretting the loss of three valuable lives and the wounds sustained by four others and he specifically commended the officers who led the shore parties, including his Serene Highness, Prince William, who was with the marines. He also wrote warmly of the Acting Commissioner, Mr St John, who volunteered to accompany the attack. His skills as an interpreter were most valuable 'as also his knowledge of the native character.'

Admiral Austen expressed his 'entire approval' of the operation, but the *Straits Times* had the final say on 9 March 1852:

> The utmost activity prevailed in the flotilla but although the stockades were carefully approached and surrounded, the pirates managed to escape unscathed, making repeated stealthy attacks as opportunity offered ... There was not the slightest indication of a man being even wounded.

The *Dolphin* murders were not avenged for another twenty-seven years when Captain Edwards in HMS *Kestrel* attacked and razed Tungku, the last of the great pirate strongholds, and destroyed sixteen armed perahu fitted out for sea. But Austen did not live to hear the news. Jane's 'particular little brother' was felled by cholera and died 'winning all hearts by his gentleness and kindness when struggling with disease.'[5] The Admiral was seventy-three and was leading his squadron up the Irrawaddy during war with Burma when he succumbed. His remains, preserved in rum, were returned for interment at Trincomalee.

Chapter XIV

'And ev'n his failings lean'd to Virtue's side.'

Robbie's death did not dispel the enmity between him and Brooke. On the contrary, their adherents regrouped and Burns's letter to Palmerston fomented the actions of the formidable Radical leader, Joseph Hume, in the Commons. Like Brooke, Hume had served in the East India Company, but as a non-combatant, and in sharp contrast, his childhood lacked the wealth and opportunity of his future adversary.

Born in Montrose, Angus, a younger son in a large family, Hume attributed his success to his mother's care, courage and sound common sense. Mrs Hume was widowed early, but her devotion to her family won their lasting honour and affection. The boy was educated in 'reading, writing, "accounts", and a smattering of Scotch Latinity' and was apprenticed to a local surgeon apothecary about the age of thirteen.[1] Hume remained with his master for three years, mainly occupied in compounding prescriptions, until he began his formal medical education in Edinburgh in 1793. He was awarded his basic surgeon's mate's diploma from the Royal College of Surgeons of that city in March 1795,[2] at the age of eighteen, but the College's Licentiateship was not then accepted by the Honourable Company for appointment as Surgeon. So, after further examination by the London College in 1797, he was appointed Assistant Surgeon in the maritime service of the East India Company. Hume made his first voyage to the East in the same year and became a full Assistant Surgeon in November 1799, when he sailed to Bengal in the *Houghton*.

Despite his humble origins, Hume did not lack powerful advocates in the Member of Parliament for Forfar, David Scott, a Director of the East India Company, and James Burnes WS, Provost of Montrose and relative of the Bard, Robert Burns. Hume's rapid acquisition of Hindustani and Persian and his flair for administration led to attachments and appointments in the Company's army, its agencies and in the commissariat, where he gained fame for his introduction of a safe means of drying gunpowder in humid, tropical climates.

In 1808, after Hume had served the Honourable Company with distinction, he returned to England having amassed an 'honestly earned fortune of £30,000 – £40,000'. Hume then spent several years in travel on the continent and in Egypt, before entering Parliament as Member for Weymouth. He never forgot his boyhood in Montrose nor the Burnes family and he assisted the Provost's third son, Alexander, to join the Honourable Company. In a short, meteoric career, this young Scot won renown as Sekundur Burnes of Afghanistan, was knighted, appointed CB and elected FRS. Both he and his younger brother were hacked to death in Kabul in 1841.

Hume had an illustrious career in the Commons where Hansard records his 'incessant political activity'. But while one biographer wrote that 'His industry and patience were almost boundless, and he was indefatigable in exposing every kind of extravagance and abuse.' St John described him as an old and obstinate man 'who dearly loved a grievance'.[3] 'By garbled extract, by untrue reports, by means which I know not,' Wise, Brooke's erstwhile agent, succeeded in gaining Hume's confidence and Brooke was vilified in the press and in the House for several years.

When Brooke returned to Sarawak in 1848 after his investiture in Singapore, he wrote to Templer:[4]

> At length an explosion is about to take place between me and friend Wise. That he has personally hated and inveterately abused me, whenever he dared, I well know, but not this or any mistake or mismanagement would have induced me to discard him, and to force him to an explanation; but it is, what appears to me, his deliberate attempt to sacrifice my interests and the interests of Sarawak.

Brooke demanded 'a full and clear explanation and a final settlement' of his accounts and placed the matter in the hands of his family's solicitor, Mr Cameron.

Wise had served as Brooke's agent from 1841 to 1848 and had gained Brooke's confidence by the standard of his work and by the trouble he took in placing his employer's letters and correspondence in the proper hands, in his dealings with the several departments of Government. Wise visited Brooke in Sarawak in 1845 when Brooke signed a covenant drawn up and written by Wise, agreeing, in effect, to divide the profits accruing from antimony ore after payment of expenses. Wise returned to England with the document and immediately began operations which Brooke considered detrimental to the development of Sarawak and at variance with the spirit of the agreement. The divergence of their views and motives is evident in their correspondence at that time and Brooke ended the arrangement in 1846.

Brooke reiterated his instructions to Wise to lease the supply of antimony ore to any London capitalists and Wise did so, with Messrs Melville and Street who lacked sufficient funds and were declared bankrupt in 1847. Wise then directed the Singapore firm of Duff and Ruppell to stop working the ore and to lay up the schooner *Julia*. Brooke was irate and indicated the consequences of Wise's folly which, among others, would ruin several hundred Indian and Chinese traders, who were totally dependent upon the ship's regular passages between Sarawak and Singapore.

In February 1850, Hume took part in a House of Commons debate on a new 'head-money' bill, designed to alter the Act of 1825 which allowed payments to captains and ships' companies for each prisoner taken at sea, for each slave recovered or for each pirate captured or killed. Hume moved that the papers on Brooke's operations against the 'pirates' of the Saribas and Sakarang rivers in 1849 should be laid before the House, before its members voted on the appropriation of £100,000 head-money, claimed under the old Act. In a subsequent debate in May, the Radical leader, Richard Cobden, questioned the payment of head-money in respect of the 1849 campaign and in July, Hume asked for an inquiry into the involvement of British forces since 1841. However, the Radical attacks faltered and failed and Brooke's explanations were accepted by Palmerston and his government.

On 20 December 1851, Joseph Hume[5] wrote to Palmerston stating that Brooke's statements in respect of Robert Burns and the Borneo mines were so contradictory to the facts of which he was aware, that he wrote to 'the identical Mr Gliddon', who replied on 25 November from Pittsburgh, Pennsylvania. Gliddon[6] commented on Brooke's letter to Palmerston of 26 May 1848, with particular reference to the sentence:

> I may mention that the Sultan of Borneo recently granted the same
> lease to a gentleman of the name of Gliddon and other parties, and
> that when he visited Bintulu, he was too happy to escape, as the

chiefs threatened to put him to death for his interference.

Gliddon was prepared to swear an affidavit 'in regard to the truth or falsity' of Brooke's assertion at Hume's request, referring to his second article on 'Trade and Piracy in the Eastern Archipelago' which was published in *Hunt's Merchant Magazine*, New York, in July 1851. Gliddon wrote that during his visit to Bruné, the Sultan granted him a ten-year lease of all the mineral wealth except coal, in the provinces of Bintulu, Tatow and Balanian. Armed with the Royal Perjanjian (an agreement tantamount to a Turkish firman or licence), Gliddon proceeded to Singapore on the *Amelia* where he chartered the *Zeelust*, and in company with John Goodridge, another American then resident in Canton, he sailed to the Bintulu river with the intention of inspecting the antimony mines. They arrived on 3 January 1848 and as the bar created problems, they anchored ten miles off. They estimated the town to be twenty-five miles distant so they took the long-boat and were received with a salute, because the chiefs said that they were the first white men ever seen in that province. Gliddon's companions left him at the second chief's house on his own for three days and he later stayed unarmed for a night before returning to the *Zeelust* with two chiefs. Gliddon continued:

> Nothing could exceed the kindness and hospitality evinced towards myself and party by the three chiefs, nor the general politeness of the resident population.

Gliddon found that the antimony ore could not be landed in Singapore for a profitable sum because of the great expense of land transport in Borneo and he had to acquaint the chiefs with the unwelcome fact that the lease granted by the Sultan could not be used to common advantage. In spite of this news, the chiefs not only expressed their disappointment but implored Gliddon to settle among them as a trader in Gutta Percha. He referred Hume to Captain Brown of the *Zeelust* and Goodridge of the House of Wetmore and Company, Canton, for corroboration of his story. Gliddon was never under the slightest apprehension during his visit to Bintulu and so far as being 'too happy to escape' as Brooke asserted, he would willingly return:

... feeling persuaded that the common humanity of the natives would shield me or anyone else who speaks their language – even from Sir James Brooke's trafficking jealousy and unscrupulous malevolences.

Gliddon then volunteered comment on Burns's letter to Palmerston which appeared in the London *Examiner* of 4 October 1851. He stated that they met twice in Bruné and on Labuan. In Bruné, Burns competed for the same antimony mines and was unsuccessful. After Gliddon abandoned the project, Burns obtained the second lease and their experiences agreed with respect to the gentle disposition of the natives to European visitors.

Indeed the only obstacle to intercourse with the Orang-Bintulu and many other Bornean tribes, emanates from the insidious artifices of Sir James Brooke himself. The agricultural and trading communities along those Bornean rivers, that are as yet uncorrupted by the example of our English Pizarro, entertain towards all persons who visit them with legitimate objects, the same kind of feelings with which the inhabitants of Sarawak welcomed the quondam Mr Brooke on his first apparition ...

Gliddon then referred to Crookshank's[7] letter of 5 January 1848 to the Chiefs of Bintulu concerning the antimony ore at Bintulu, which Burns mentioned in the *Examiner*. About August 1847, Mr Brooke took passage in the *Nemesis* to Singapore for England while Gliddon remained in Sarawak. Suddenly the *Nemesis* returned and the mailbag was immediately brought to Brooke's counting-house and opened in the presence of Messrs Hentig, Ruppell and Crookshank:

A despatch from Mr Brooke, marked 'private and strictly confidential', directed to Mr A. Crookshank (Police Magistrate and general sbirro) was immediately seized upon.

He read it with some perturbation, and pocketed it, observing considerable mystery on the subject.

I was much amused when, the next day, Mr Brooke's Malayan Secretary coming as was his wont, to pay me his morning visit, and chat familiarly over affairs of the nation in general and his individual troubles in particular, told me that he had been writing a letter under Mr Crookshank's dictation, to the Bintulu chiefs, threatening them with his master's condign vengeance if they suffered any *orang puti* [white men] to explore the antimony mines, or even to reside in that province. Within a few hours this scrap of intelligence received confirmation from European sources, coupled with the remark that the approaching north-east monsoon would retard the transmission of the said letter to Bintulu for some time.

Two or three days after this, the steamer *Phlegethon* arrived. She brought me a letter from Mr Henry Wise ... notifying my dismissal. Wishing, in consequence, to anticipate Mr Crookshank's police machinations, I left in the *Phlegethon* for Bruné; obtained a lease of those identical mines from the Sultan; went to Singapore; effected arrangements with Messrs C. J. Perry and J. Harvey Weed; sailed for Bintulu as before narrated; found to our general regret and loss, that we could not work them profitably, and had abandoned the scheme long before Mr Brooke's imbecile veto upon independent commerce reached the Bintulu chiefs for whom it was destined. Mr Burns, who followed me, does not appear to have been so fortunate.

Meanwhile in Singapore, the *Straits Times* edited by R. C. Woods echoed the clamour against Brooke and his administration from its first publication of the *Dolphin* murders. On 18 May 1852, the paper carried an editorial headed 'The Late Mr Robert Burns and his Detractors', a sustained irony, in which it was stated that the *Straits Times* would shortly publish Burns's letter to Lord Palmerston and show its readers:

... in its true light the honesty and justice of Sir James Brooke. Indeed poor Burns' whole career out in these seas remains a standing monument of Brooke's liberal and enlightened policy. Let us glance over once again the facts of the case, and see how they stand the light.

In 1847 a good deal of attention, for various reasons, became directed to the Bintuloo mines. A mercantile house of high standing in Glasgow, and its correspondents in Singapore, determined upon seeing whether the Antimony there could not be worked profitably, and whether it were possible to open out in this way and by degrees the resources of that part of the coast of Borneo. Poor Burns, who was then without employment in Singapore, was engaged by the representative of this association here to proceed to Bintuloo and see what could be done towards effecting this desirable object.

He [Burns] was known to be a man of indomitable energy, well acquainted with the country to which he had previously paid a lengthy visit, and of unquestionable integrity. Moreover on his former trips he had been well received by the natives, and had succeeded in acquiring some smattering of their language. He was accordingly, as we have said, selected as the person best qualified to undertake the matter in hand, and he was sent down in a small vessel to Bintuloo in June of the same year. Here he remained some months during which period he not only succeeded in conciliating the good will and securing the respect of the chief, but actually obtained from the Rajah, a promise of the lease of the mines and the hand of his daughter in marriage.

In the meantime Sir James Brooke, always jealous and distrustful of the Bintuloo expedition – as likely to affect seriously the Antimony monopoly he enjoyed at Sarawak – became so sensibly alarmed at the continued success of poor Burns that he determined to leave no means untried of turning him out of the country. To effect this, to him exceedingly desirable object, he accordingly had recourse in the first instance to intimidation – first frightening Burns' employers into requesting him to leave Bintuloo at once, at whatever loss of time or money, and subsequently himself threatening the native Chieftain that in the event of his allowing any white man to settle in the country, he would come down and destroy and exterminate him and his people. Finding however that neither threats nor entreaties would serve his cause, and that Burns still continued unmoveable, Brooke at last determined upon taking one of those extraordinary steps which, perfectly unscrupulous as he is, he only now and then has recourse to, and as Her Majesty's Commissioner in Borneo, ordered a war steamer at once to proceed to Bintuloo and bring Burns away by force if he would not come of his own accord. His orders were obeyed and Burns was brought off in the steamer, and ultimately reached Singapore. At the latter place he indited a very interesting account of the Kayans of Bintuloo which was pub-

lished in the *Journal of the Indian Archipelago*; here also he wrote
the letter to Viscount Palmerston now moved for by Mr Hume, and
here he continued occasionally making trading voyages on the coast
of Borneo, until the time of his most melancholy murder.

Such, without one word of exaggeration are the facts of the case
which it is the object of Mr Hume's motion to expose, and such the
manner in which Sir James Brooke makes use of the power conferred on him in his public capacity to further his private ends. Let it
not be supposed, however, that this is the only instance of the persecution which anyone adventurous enough to act as Burns did, may
expect to meet with at the hands of Her Majesty's Commissioner of
Borneo. Even with regard to *him* it was only one of a thousand.

The article continued:

Sometime subsequently to this occurrence a case came on in the
Court of Labuan in which Burns was concerned. Mr Napier, the
Judge, decided the matter in Burns' favor, and stated that the opposition party had not a leg to stand upon. A few months after this –
shortly after the removal of Mr Napier from his Lieutenant-
Governorship – Brooke, with his old grudge against Burns still
ungratified, hearing of the affair, and conceiving that he could now
annoy his enemy, requested Mr Scott – the acting Lieutenant-
Governor – to issue a warrant for the apprehension of Burns, and to
commit him to jail in the very same case which had already been
tried and decided upon by Mr Napier. This was done, and the original warrant lies before us as we write. Nay, even after death, Brooke
has still pursued his enemy and slanders him dead as he did living.

The editorial refers to another matter which is discussed elsewhere and
concludes that:

Such are a few of the facts connected with this matter, – facts on
which we challenge contradiction or reply. We do not relate them
here from any wish to open up old grievances. We know that people
are heartily sick of Brooke and Borneo. Being entrusted by Burns
with all his private papers, on his last quitting Singapore, for the pur-

pose of repelling slanders which he felt persuaded Brooke would shower upon him when absent, we perform but duty to his memory, our bounden duty, now that he is no more, by rescuing him from the polluted and polluting hands of men who sacrifice every principle of humanity to forward their pecuniary interests; and so long as the Rajah of Sarawak, not as Rajah but as Her Majesty's Commissioner, and his satellites continue to abuse the powers entrusted to them by Government, to serve their own private ends; so long as calumny, falsehood and garbling are made use of to attempt to deceive the public, so will we, at whatever cost to ourselves, expose and denounce them.

Chapter XV

'Intrigues half-gather'd, conversation-scraps ...'

Hume wrote to the Earl of Malmesbury on 7 April 1852.[1]

I FEEL it to be a public duty, in the prosecution of my efforts to disabuse the public of the strange and discreditable delusions of which it has been so long the victim, to submit to you some strictures on the series of confident but unproved assertions made by Sir James Brooke, as contained in the Borneo Correspondence presented to the House of Commons on the 23rd of March, 1852.

Mr Robert Burns can no longer avail himself of the opportunity afforded him by your Lordship's predecessor, of refuting the assertions against his character made by Sir James Brooke. He has fallen a victim to the piracy of tribes not natives of Borneo, and close to the locality in which Sir James Brooke had declared piracy to have been extirpated in 1846. Sir James Brooke makes various allegations against the reputation of the late Mr Burns, which, as they are unaccompanied by evidence of the slightest validity, must, until evidence be adduced, be viewed as no better than calumnies. By way of testimony, Sir James produces the translations of the letters of three chiefs of the Bintulu Dyaks, two of which make no allusion whatever to Mr Burns, while in the third he is basely charged with 'taking men's wives' without their consent, and advising the killing of all strangers who entered their rivers.

In the absence of any real evidence, recourse is had to the loose and unsupported allegations contained in Sir James Brooke's letter to the Bintulu chiefs, in which it is insinuated that Mr Burns committed crimes; cheated; traded unfairly; that he offered opinions respecting the Government of the country; that he intrigued and spread false reports; &c., &c. Such vagaries are hardly worth the trouble of refutation ...

Sir James Brooke states that the question of working the antimony mines having been referred to him by Her Majesty's late Ministers, he 'strongly objected to British subjects obtaining exclusive grants in aid of their commercial projects, and carrying on trade, backed by a firman, to the injury of the natives.

This bold conclusion appears to my mind a striking proof of the extent to which the false position in which he stands has blinded Sir James Brooke. While he was thus arbitrating on the claims of others, he was himself most flagrantly violating the very principle, he here lays down.

Given those circumstances, Hume was at a loss to understand how Brooke:

... should be considered by Government immaculate and above suspicion, while the evidence of all other English traders is rejected as being actuated by corrupt motives; and therefore unworthy of credit or acceptance.

He had not only monopolized the ore of Antimony in Sarawak, but he had, even when holding the office of Her Majesty's Commissioner, obtained an exclusive grant from the Sultan of Borneo of all the ascertained coal-fields within his dominions to himself and his heirs forever. I must indeed express my astonishment and regret, at finding that Her Majesty's Advisers, should ever have referred to the arbitration, or even consulted the opinion, of one whose position rendered him so obviously amenable to the suspicion of being governed by interested motives, on a question which required an unbiassed and impartial arbiter.

Hume then continued to offer his observations on:

... the real nature of his tenure of this principality which is now for the first time made known to the Public, through the document, which bears the signatures of Mr James Motley and the late Mr Burns ...

In Singapore, meanwhile, R. C. Woods of the *Straits Times* continued his defence of Burns and his assaults on Brooke. On 25 May 1852, the newspaper published a letter written on 18 September the previous year, by William Napier the former Lieutenant-Governor of Labuan to Walter Scott Duncan, a Scots merchant of Singapore.

Napier had no difficulty in stating that while he was Lieutenant-Governor during Burns's residence in Labuan, nothing occurred that gave Napier occasion to form an unfavourable impression of him. Although he heard more than once and he himself believed that Burns 'evinced much warmth of temper in his transactions and discussions with his countrymen there', Napier heard nothing regarding his general conduct on Labuan that was open to reproach. Napier's personal dealings with Burns during the period in question were wholly of an official nature and related to his projects on the coast and his intention of revisiting Bintulu and Kayan territory. When Burns requested the native Nakhodahs who were willing to give him passage in their perahus, there was no objection to their doing so.

These people, so far as I saw, professed a readiness to receive Mr Burns on board, and seemed to entertain the very reverse feelings of personal objection to him. One of these men, Nakhoda Gadore, on coming to pay his respects after his return from a trading voyage, in which he had been accompanied by Mr Burns, highly commended his conduct and deportment during the time they were together, saying, that although it was a small vessel, Mr Burns was neither vexed nor angry, that he ate and drank like one of themselves, and was very different from what the Pangeran Jalludeen had reported. This Pangeran was one of those provided by the Sultan to escort Mr Burns to Bintuloo on his first visit there and who reported of Mr Burns very unfavourably to Sir James Brooke – the said Pangeran himself having invariably received the worst character possible from Sir James Brooke.

With respect to the dispute between Nakhoda Jalludeen and Mr Burns, to which you alluded, it is only a mere act of justice to the latter to mention the following facts as they came within my judicial cognizance.

In the month of May 1849, and if I remember rightly, during the few days Sir J. Brooke was on the island, on his way to Sooloo, I caused a summons to be issued, from the General Court of Labuan, at the suit of Nakhoda Jalludeen, against Mr Burns, to recover the sum of $22 or thereabouts, as the value of certain goods sold and delivered. On the day of the return of the Summons, Mr Burns did not appear and information was sent that he was too ill to attend, which I thought proper to obtain confirmation of, and found that he was labouring under an attack of fever and ague. The Plaintiff Jalludeen was present, and was told to appear, either the following day, or some other early day named, for the trial of the cause. On the day thus appointed, Mr Burns did and Jalludeen did not appear: and I was informed (by Mr Low according to my recollection) that the Plaintiff had left the Island and gone back to Borneo.

He never again appeared to prosecute his suit; which it could not be said he wanted opportunity of doing, because before the Summons was issued, Mr Burns had resided for two months in Labuan without interruption, and continued to do so afterwards with brief intervals of absence until the middle of the following November when he left the island in the barque *Polka* on a trading voyage to the Northward. Of the merits of the question at issue I could not pronounce definitively in a judicial sense, not having had it properly before me; but from what I heard Jalludeen himself state on the occasion it appeared to me that Mr Burns had just grounds for resisting the claim made against him, and putting it to the issue of a judicial determination.

I conclude with observing that I consider the language in which Sir James Brooke denounces Mr Burns to the native chiefs as only too likely to be construed into incitement to acts of violence and wrong: and that the course which as apparent from the parliamentary papers, he considers himself justified in pursuing towards that young man, is much to be regretted; virtually amounting, as it must do, in the eyes of all who know the Malay character, and the power and influence Sir James Brooke has been enabled to exercise on the coast of Borneo, to a mere persecution, the effects of which I hope and trust Mr Burns may find the means of counteracting.

I have the honor to be,
Your most Obedient Servant,
Wm. Napier
Late Lt. Governor of Labuan
To W.S. Duncan Esq.

Napier's letter is manifestly honest and he cannot be accused of collusion with the anti-Brooke faction, despite his treatment by the Raja. On 20 November 1849, the *Straits Times* reported that:

> The Lieutenant Governor appears happy in the art of estranging all of whose unfortunate lot it is to live under his rule. To former vagaries we have now to add the arrest of the amiable and gallant commandant of the military force, Captain McCaskill.

There followed a letter from 'Veritas,' a resident of Labuan, who stated that when this officer obeyed an order from his superior to return to Singapore, he was arrested on Napier's command and charged with attempting to leave the island without permission of the Lieutenant-Governor. 'Veritas' continued:

> All the officials have quarrelled with him and pass him by without recognition, the agents of the Eastern Archipelago Co., working the coal mines are at variance with him. The noses of the military officers turn heavenward whenever his name is mentioned ...

Brooke,[2] depressed, wrote:

> I have had a good deal to disquiet me ... disappointment in the Lieut. Governor of Labuan – who whenever I leave that place gets into a dilemma ...

Then a few weeks later, on Christmas Eve 1849, Brooke sent Napier the Petition of James Riley,[3] who ran the 'spirit farm'. The document contained a list of allegations, principally that Napier had a business connection with Meldrum, his office clerk, and had allowed him to engage in trade and as a partner in the 'spirit farm'. It was also alleged that the Lieutenant-Governor favoured Meldrum and used his official influence to advance Meldrum's trading venture, 'contrary to every principle and usage of Her Majesty's service'.

The accusations evoked massive popular support on Napier's behalf. Prominent European inhabitants of Singapore, mostly the principal merchants, signed a petition in his favour. Another, in translation, emanated from 'the Bazarman and labouerers now residing in Labuan' and Burns was a signatory to a document submitted by a group of traders and residents. Nicol and others declared that they knew of no trading connection between Napier and Meldrum. While Woods, the Editor of the *Straits Times*, to whom 'Veritas' had addressed his letter, wrote to the Lieutenant-Governor informing him that he had not printed the entire correspondence. The reason was that Woods believed Napier was not:

> ... capable of any such petty and contemptible act. I remember perfectly well that early in November, after the receipt of the letter alluded to, I mentioned in Messrs. Dare and Co.'s store, by way of a joke, that a new firm had started at Labuan under the style of Napier, Meldrum and Co. Captain Wallage of the *Nemesis*, and others were present on that occasion and I think that everyone understood the allusion to be merely a joke and since then I have not heard more of the matter.

'Veritas' also claimed that Burns had recently been employed by Napier in secret negotiations with the Pangerans and Nakhodas to work the coal in the Rejang region and that Burns had returned in mid-September with an Orang Kaya and his suite, to visit Napier concerning a speculation in tobacco.

The appeals were to no avail. Earl Grey and his government in Britain upheld Brooke's actions and Napier was dismissed in 1850. On 31 January 1851, Napier wrote to Earl Grey:

> Your Lordship will not refuse to allow that a consideration of the mischief which may be occasioned by the slanders which may be raised in a small settlement like Labuan, by one evil-disposed person, will suffice of itself to account for the assistance I afforded to Mr Meldrum being misconstrued.

Emily Hahn and Tarling, two of Brooke's recent biographers, believed that Napier was probably innocent, another victim of the Raja's penchant for overkill.

On 22 April 1852, St John[4] wrote to Brooke:

I mentioned some months since the intrigues that were being carried on by Mr Motley, in Borneo, and the malicious reports he was spreading to your prejudice along the north-west coast.

Motley was Superintendent of the Eastern Archipelago Company. Before he visited the Baram territory in June 1851, St John called at Bruné in the *Pluto* where he learned from 'many respectable natives and from several of the Pangerans, that Mr Motley had informed them that you [Brooke] had been recalled in disgrace.' Motley was also alleged to have said that the British Government was so dissatisfied with Brooke's conduct that he would never again be entrusted with authority in these seas and that he told the same story to the chiefs along the north-west coast.

St John reminded Brooke that he would be well aware:

... that native nobles in telling you such news always soften it as much as possible, and this they certainly did on the present occasion. Were a private individual to have spread such false reports, it would have been immaterial, but Mr Motley is looked upon by the natives as the representative of a company; and as he always gives himself out to be a very great man, as in fact 'a Tuan Besar', his word is supposed to be worth consideration.

In his next visit to Bruné in August, St John learned that Motley was boasting that the Sultan was writing letters to the British Government complaining of Brooke's conduct towards him. St John thought that it would be worthwhile broaching the topic with Makota who denied that the Bruné Government would ever have considered such behaviour, strongly protesting that they had no complaint whatever against Brooke. St John was convinced from some of Makota's expressions that Motley and Burns had been attempting to intrigue with Government officials.

St John found some notes written by Burns in the course of business and claimed that a few days prior to his visit, Burns had endeavoured to persuade the Sultan, Pangeran Moumein and others to write to the Queen about Brooke. Furthermore, Motley was said to have offered two hundred dollars for a letter relating to Brooke's affairs. Makota also told St John that Burns had been giving presents to the Sultan and that he had invited Ministers to a feast on board his boat and had given presents to each. Such conduct was so unusual for Burns that it raised the suspicions of the Sultan and his government. The letter was apparently so important to Motley that, had he obtained it, he would have immediately gone to Singapore. St John concluded by stating that Makota had informed the Labuan Government of Motley's machinations and of his attempts to bribe the Bornean officials and that he would not be surprised if Hume did not come forward with a letter purporting to have been written by the Sultan:

> A heavy bribe given to some of the inferior nobles about the Palace would induce them surreptitiously to obtain the Sultan's seal.

On 11 October 1852, Brooke[5] wrote from Surrey to the Earl of Malmesbury stating that:

> In consequence of the proceedings of Mr Motley, the Superintendent of the Eastern Archipelago Company, and the late Mr Robert Burns, I addressed a letter on the subject to the Sultan and Rajahs of Borneo, the answer to which, with a translation, I have now the honour to inclose.
>
> If the Government of Borneo is to be credited, the statements contained in the letter addressed to Mr Hume by Mr Motley and Mr Burns, were fabricated by these two persons for their own purposes.
>
> The details of this conspiracy have already been laid before Parliament, and I may leave Her Majesty's Government to infer the consequences of a public Company, incorporated by Royal Charter, being involved in such transactions.

Sir James Brooke[6] to the Sultan of Borneo, Pangeran Muda Mahomed, Pangeran Muda Moumein, Pangeran Indra Makota, and the Rajahs of Bruné.

Inclosure 1 in No. 8

It has come to our knowledge that some wicked persons have, since our departure, been often in Bruné, spreading false reports, and endeavouring to persuade the Sultan to write to the Queen of England concerning our proceedings; and that they have been offering money and making promises to induce the Sultan to do this.

On this account we write to our friends, to demand that they will inform us, by letter, of the names of all such persons, and the names of the persons in England, whom they have mentioned as desiring this.

We write this openly and from a true heart, knowing that our friends wish to do right, and will not conceal the authors of this slander; and that they will inform us fully of the state of the case, as it now stands, so as not to keep a wickedness concealed, which will bring shame on all concerned, and make a blot upon our friendship which has lasted so long.

Brooke's letter was delivered by Low and the Sultan[7] and two Pangerans replied, denying any knowledge of the intrigue, 'as we do not heed what is not good.'

Inclosure 2 in No. 8

Regarding Mr Motley, he formally came to us, having no business whatever beyond wishing to meet us, and he presented us with six muskets. He came afterwards to Bruné, and again came there on the business of the agreement concerning the coal.

Regarding Mr Burns, he came in a schooner, and requested us to let him see our friend's (Brooke's) letter addressed to the Orang Kaya Pamancha of Bintulu. We answered, of what use was that letter (to him), we have it not, nor do we know anything about it. Burns strongly begged for that letter, and he promised to give dollars for it, because he wanted to copy and send it to Mr Napier.

Mr Burns likewise informed us that if the Sultan wished, there was one choice; if he wished to send a letter to the Queen, Mr Motley could forward it to Europe, his Company was in Europe; Mr Wise could forward it to the Queen.

When Mr Burns told us this, Mr Motley was in Borneo with him. What Mr Burns told us we heard, but did not attend to; – we thought that had we desired to send a letter to our friend the Queen, or to our friend (Brooke), what use our giving it to any other person, as we could send it to Labuan, to the Court of our friend.

This is what we know, and other than this, we do not know, but should we hear further concerning this matter, we will of course inform our friend of it.

We send no mark (of friendship) to our friend, but our compliments.

On the last day of 1851, the Foreign Secretary, Earl Granville, acknowledged Brooke's letter to Palmerston of 2 December, on the matter of Burns's lease from the Sultan of Borneo to exploit the minerals of Bintulu and Burns's complaints of the measures adopted by Brooke. Copies of a letter from Burns and extracts of that from Gliddon to Hume were enclosed. On the same day, Mr Addington of the Foreign Office, was instructed by Granville to acknowledge receipt of Burns's letter to Palmerston of 28 June. The communication addressed to 'Robert Burns Esqr., Singapore' was never delivered. Burns was dead.

Brooke, in London, replied to Granville on 5 January 1852[8] stating that he had already commented upon Burns's letter of '2nd [sic] June 1851' and 'Having only seen Mr Burns' letter in the public papers, I should not have considered it necessary to notice the allegations it contained', had he not been advised to do so in anticipation of what Hume might say in the House of Commons.

Brooke continued:

There appears, therefore, to be some misapprehension in forwarding to me, for my observations, a letter to which I have already replied; and viewing my reply as unconnected with Mr Burns' communication to Lord Palmerston, which has been so warmly espoused by Mr Hume.

Should Her Majesty's Government now desire to obtain further information on this subject, or consider it proper to forward my reply to Mr Burns for his additional observations, I would suggest that a reference should be likewise made to Mr Nicol, a gentleman of character, of the firm of Messrs. Hamilton, Gray, and Co., in whose behalf Mr Burns was acting at Bintulu; to the Lieutenant-Governor of Labuan; and to the police office of that settlement.

Any complaint should in propriety emanate from the partner of the firm in Singapore, who was the principal in the transactions, rather than from a subordinate or clerk, employed to carry on the business at Bintulu, and whose interest could be involved but in a very slight degree, independently of his employers.

The character of the complainant and the nature of his complaints may thus be ascertained without a tedious correspondence; and as I have already stated in my previous despatch, the copies of the official documents relating to Mr Burns will shortly be transmitted to Her Majesty's Government, to substantiate the statements I have advanced.

Brooke disparaged Gliddon's assertion that he was never in danger at Bintulu and wrote that the latter's comments:

... did not obviate the objection to British subjects obtaining exclusive rights over extensive and unknown provinces, for the purposes of mercantile speculation.

Brooke also dissented from Gliddon:

... on the safety of residing and trading amongst any Malay community subject to an arbitrary government and not under the control of settled laws: but on the contrary, I am convinced from history and my own experience, that trade carried on under Malayan rule has ever been precarious and unsafe, and that exactly in proportion that it is coerced by the rulers, does it become a curse to the poorer classes.

In the case of Mr Gliddon I entertain no doubt that the mandate which he held from the Sovereign of Borneo was as acceptable to the Rayas [sic] of Bintulu, as the firman of the Ottoman Sultan usually is to a Greek community; and that it would have been exercised with equal justice and moderation.

To save your Lordship trouble, the previous refutation of Mr Burns's statement may suffice to refute those set forth by Mr Gliddon; and one example will show the nature of the latter person's evidence. Mr Burns writes that a letter signed 'A. Crookshank', arrived at Bintulu from Sarawak in the month of March 1848; and Mr Gliddon to throw 'a glimmering light' on this point, for Mr Hume's guidance, asserts that a letter of precisely the same tenure was written by Mr Crookshank's order in June, or early in July of 1847, the former being the month that I left Sarawak on my return to England.

Upon the testimony of these two persons, apart from their voluminous opinions on public affairs, it is proved that their intercourse with Bintulu was not prevented; that the antimony ore could not be profitably worked; and consequently that there could be no object on my part in checking the schemes of speculators, excepting when called upon to do so by a sense of public duty.

Brooke repeated that he objected strongly and that his objections were shared by the late Lord Auckland and he believed by the rest of Her Majesty's Ministers:

> ... to British subjects obtaining exclusive grants in aid of their commercial projects, and carrying on trade, backed by a firman, to the injury of the natives.
>
> Your Lordship is aware that in every part of the world there are persons to be found who require the restraint of authority when they wander beyond the pale of the laws; and that such persons are always ready, when encouraged by a Member of Parliament, to charge upon an executive officer the results of their own vices and imprudence.
>
> Better would it be to abandon our settlements and our trade in those seas, and to leave the native population to its miseries, and its own wild sense of justice, than to expose it to the unrestrained licence of European speculators, and to the barbarities of piratical hordes, supported by their friends and advocates in the House of Commons.
>
> Mr Gliddon has informed his correspondent that he was dismissed from his situation by Mr Wise, and I may add, that it was in consequence of his not evincing that anxiety in pecuniary affairs for which Mr Hume was once so remarkable. Mr Gliddon subsequently became a constable in Singapore, and again losing his situation, retired to America.
>
> It is necessary to be acquainted with the conduct of a witness in the ordinary transactions of life, in order to appreciate the value of his testimony; and in positions even the most exalted, a gentleman's character may be fairly judged by that of his correspondents and associates.

The course pursued by Mr Hume in heaping accusations – alike the most grave and the most frivolous – upon a public officer, year after year, may confidently be left to the judgment of every man of integrity and right feeling; and although I feel that I am subjected to an unprecedented persecution from this gentleman, I shall continue to discharge the duties entrusted to me, so long as I deem it to be consistent with my own honour and advantageous to the position and commerce of this country in the Eastern Seas.

Three weeks later, Brooke[9] wrote again to Granville, enclosing a translation of a letter from Makota[10] which had been passed to him by Scott, the Lieutenant-Governor of Labuan. Makota stated that Motley and Burns offered three hundred dollars for the letter concerning Brooke's affairs. Brooke also observed that:

The capture of the schooner *Dolphin*, and the massacre of her crew, will prove that the caution I in vain endeavoured to inculcate was not needless; and I regret to add that on the recapture of this vessel, it was discovered that her cargo comprised a considerable quantity of fire-arms and gunpowder!

At the same time, Mr Burns's log or journal came into the possession of Mr St John, the Acting Commissioner, and an entry was found, that at the instigation of the murdered man, the Sultan had promised to make a complaint against my proceedings.

Any comment would be superfluous; though it is sufficiently interesting to observe the machinery by which the yearly staple of Parliamentary charges is manufactured in the East; and at all times an appeal to the cupidity and evil passions of the native rulers will produce as many complaints as Mr Hume could himself desire. On my part I am content to leave the facts to the judgement of honest men.

On 12 February 1852, Brooke[11] submitted various papers in corroboration of the statements contained in his 'previous despatches relative to the late Mr Burns'. The first[12] dealt with Burns's application to Admiral Inglefield in February, 1848, for confirmation of the Sultan's lease to work the mines at Bintulu. The latter referred the matter to the Lords Commissioners of the Admiralty who recommended:

... the Sultan to suspend all concessions until the arrival of Mr Brooke, who will convey to him the sentiments of Her Majesty's Government as to the precautions and limitations with which exclusive privileges should be granted, if granted at all.

Brooke[13] also enclosed a statement from Mr C. D'Oyley H. Aplin, who was a member of the Bench of Magistrates when he lived on Labuan, in response to Brooke's request for an account of complaints against Burns by the crew of his trading vessel. Aplin was in London, without ready access to the official records of the police court in Labuan, so he trusted to memory.

Burns twice appeared before the Bench, the first time in July or August 1850, on his return from a trading voyage to Bintulu. The captain of the vessel of which Burns was super-cargo, charged that the latter had violently assaulted him and attempted to assume command at Bintulu. On another occasion during that passage, Burns allegedly threatened the skipper to compel him to enter the Baram River, although the surf on the bar was so high that the Master swore that the little ship would have been lost. It was claimed that Burns struck the skipper on the side with a cutlass, but those of the crew who were called as witnesses seemed so alarmed that they could not swear to have seen a blow delivered. However, they saw Burns on the after-deck, 'brandishing the sword and daring one to come aft'. Burns denied the assault, claiming that he had seized the weapon as he expected to be attacked by the captain with whom he had exchanged 'high words.'

The case was dismissed because of unsatisfactory evidence and because both parties acknowledged that they had quarrelled before. Both were reproved for their disgraceful conduct and for setting a bad example to the crew who were unanimous in stating that Burns displayed a violent temper and frequently ill-treated them.

On the second occasion, some six months later, Burns himself was the plaintiff and he charged the captain with assault and driving him off the boat at night, while she lay at anchor in Labuan harbour. There was no light aboard, the crew were asleep and there was no evidence as to the origin of the scuffle, 'which ended in Mr Burns' precipitate retreat', and his application to a magistrate for protection. The matter was duly heard at the police court:

... but both parties eventually agreed to arrange the business, by the captain giving up the vessel to the sole charge of Mr Burns, on consideration of being paid the full amount of his wages.

Aplin concluded his letter by stating that:

It was at this time that complaints arrived at Labuan from the Barram chiefs, of Mr Burns' disgraceful and outrageous behaviour to them whilst trading in their river, and receiving every kindness and attention; being the first white man they had seen: and it was reported, that had it not been for a contrary impression produced by your name in that part of the world, and that they could confidently appeal to you for redress and protection, Mr Burns would certainly have lost his head on that occasion.

Brooke[14] later included extracts from Burns's journal which was found by St John aboard the *Dolphin* when she was recovered.

July 30, 1851 – Mr Motley came [from] Coal Point today, and wishing to go to Bruné with me, said he offered the Sultan $200 for the Bintulu letter.

August 4th – Got the Sultan and Moumein &c., to promise to write to the Queen about Sir James Brooke and Sarawak, in two or three days.

In addition, Brooke had acquired a statement prepared by Burns and Motley on board the *Dolphin* at anchor below Pulo Chermin on the Bruné River. The date was 5 August 1851.

On the 4th of August, 1851, in the audience-hall of his Palace at Bruné, His Highness Omar Ali Sufideen, Sultan of Bruné, made to us, James Motley and Robert Burns, the following statements, in the presence and hearing of Pangeran Moumein, Prime Minister of Bruné, Pangeran Makota, Pangeran Budrudeen, and his secretary, Mohamet:

First. That in consideration of His Highness the Sultan of Bruné having made to him a grant of the territory of Sarawak, to be held

under the suzerainté of the said Sultan of Bruné, Sir James, then Mr
Brooke, agreed to and executed a bond or document, binding himself to pay yearly to His Highness the Sultan of Brunei the sum of
two thousand dollars ($2000) in the way of rent or vassalage for the
said territory of Sarawak.

The second statement alleged that when the city of Bruné was
attacked by Her Majesty's forces, about two years after the date of the said
bond or document and during the time that the Sultan was a fugitive from
his capital, Mr Brooke demanded restitution of the document. The Sultan
believed that Brooke was the sole leader of the attack and that he was acting as the representative of Queen Victoria and instructed by her. The document was therefore surrendered and no part of the annual payment had
been paid since that time nor was the document ever returned to the Sultan.

Motley and Burns asserted further that no revenues had been received
by the Sultan from any of the rivers or districts that lay between Sarawak
and the Rejang. Furthermore, when the Sultan's tax-collectors visited
those areas, the Malay inhabitants refused tribute, claiming that the
Government of Sarawak instructed them to disregard the Sultan's orders.

The fourth statement claimed that when Sir James visited Bruné on
board the *Nemesis* in December 1850, he obtained an order from the Sultan
authorising him to collect revenues between Sarawak and the Rejang on
behalf of His Highness. But no money had been paid to Bruné nor had the
Sultan received any communication on the subject, yet Brooke's agents
had established friendships with the local chiefs in the name of Sarawak's
English Raja. The Sultan was extremely anxious to recall his authority,
being persuaded that Brooke had procured the order 'with some further
and sinister motives'.

Finally, Motley and Burns affirmed that the Sultan had been led to suppose that Brooke's authority and jurisdiction on the coast of Borneo were
absolute and without appeal. Because of this, His Highness had made no
complaint, but having been more correctly informed (presumably by Motley
and Burns), he had 'for some time entertained the idea of writing to his
friend and ally Her Majesty The Queen of England,' appealing for redress.
However, he was discouraged from so doing by the fear of Brooke's
vengeance 'and by the apprehension that his letter might be intercepted.'

Chapter XVI

'Nature's law,
That man was made to mourn.'

W hen Burns left Glasgow in 1846, there was unimaginable degradation among the indigent, especially the immigrant Irish.The steady flow of seasonal labour that had persisted for years, became a torrent when they came to dig canals, excavate docks and construct railways at the start of the Industrial Revolution. But when the 'Great Hunger' savaged Ireland's population, the torrent became a flood that engulfed Liverpool and Glasgow, the second major port of entry. The destitute quickly learned that they would not be allowed to die of starvation once across the Irish Sea; while illness and inanition precluded work, the Poor Law permitted outdoor relief in most districts. By December 1846, six months after the *Princess Royal* left for Singapore, Glasgow was overrun by Irish beggars swept ashore by the unwelcome tide. In Scotland, when the Duke of Cumberland 'with bloody hands ripped the entire fabric of Highland society to shreds in 1746,'[1] the Highland Clearances began and enforced migration was exacerbated when able-bodied men and women forsook the croft and thronged to the industrial Lowlands in search of work. In 1845, readers of *The Times*[2] were reminded of the misery and penury induced by the systematic clearances in Sutherland twenty-five years before, when the population of Glen Calvie in Easter Ross, was evicted 'without a hope or prospect for the future'. While overseas trade prospered and Glasgow flourished, parts of the city gave new meaning to the expression 'abject poverty'.

At the family home on a freezing winter's day in 1852, Robbie's sister had just opened the shop when Donald Maclean, a neighbouring butcher, entered in an icy blast. 'Dear me, Donald, whit brings ye oot on sic a day?' The butcher lacked his customary cheerfulness, as he asked, 'Hae ye seen the *Courier*? A Robert Burns has been murdert oot East!' Robbie's sister paled and clutched the counter, moaning, 'No, dear God, no!' Donald led her to the back kitchen where the rest of the family had gathered, drawn by the clatter of the butcher's boots on the stone floor. They were desolated. Robbie could not be dead! His last letter from Labuan said that he was well, apart from occasional attacks of 'fever' which were common in that part of the world. He was soon to set out on another trading voyage that promised greater profits than he had dreamed of and he wrote of his friends, Borneo and how much he missed the family.

On 22 January 1852, the *Glasgow Courier* announced under the heading, 'Piracy and Slaughter in the Indian Archipelago' that 'Mr Burns, a grandson of the Scotch Poet was dead.' Next day, the Glasgow *Herald* quoted from the London *Times* that 'Mr Burns, namesake and descendant of the Poet, had died.'

When the family recovered sufficiently from the initial impact of their loss, they were perplexed. What could they do? What had become of Robbie's possessions? What of his boat? Did he leave any money? Where could they obtain more information? At length they wrote to Matthew, who by this time was in California.

After Robbie left Glasgow, the younger boy so missed his brother and longed to follow him that he enlisted in the army when he heard that a cavalry regiment would shortly join the East India Company's forces in Bengal. He became a more than competent horseman, learned to handle side-arms and in a skirmish, when he was called to assist the Regimental Surgeon, he was found to possess 'a good pair of hands'. The result was assignment as a Surgeon's Assistant when the need arose. Like Robbie, Matthew was bright and soon acquired a rudimentary knowledge of medicine and surgery, assisting at the amputation of appendages from fingertips to entire lower limbs.

But Trooper Burns was far from content. Sweating profusely in his heavy uniform in the relentless heat, amidst the filth and ever-present dangers of disease and surprise attack, he saw few prospects of advancement and none of making money. The opportunity came in 1850, when he learned of the discovery of gold in California the previous year, while stationed in Calcutta. Off-duty, one evening in the bazaar, he fell in with the First Mate of a clipper which had lost several crew on its outward voyage, so Matthew deserted and signed on for the return to San Francisco.

While California was infinitely preferable to India, Matthew, like many others, found that prospecting was far from profitable and after borrowing money from a Mr Charles Morrill, he decamped for Oregon Territory. It was here that he received his sister's letter with its news of Robbie's death.

Chapter XVII

The Search for Burns

W ho was this Robert Burns and what was his relationship to the Bard? The few primary sources of information which were available at the start of this undertaking were soon exhausted. Brooke's nineteenth-century biographers failed to mention Burns or reiterated the views of Keppel, St John and Brooke that he was a 'disreputable adventurer'. The History Centre and the Bureau of Language and Literature in Brunei Darussalam[1] contained only one reference and that was *The Pirate Wind* by Owen Rutter which first triggered this enquiry. The search was widened, initially by correspondence. For example, the Dunfermline Carnegie Library[2] consulted the *Genealogical Memoirs of the Family of Robert Burns* by Charles Rodgers (1877) and *Ancestors, Descendants and Collateral Relatives* by Robert Duthie (1859), from which it was evident that many descendants of the Bard joined the Colonial Service and many were named Robert. But as the quest intensified, its ramifications widened and the subject grew more remote: Burns was an enigma.

According to *Burns Direct Descendants* published in the *Burns Chronicle* in 1894[3] and 1895,[4] the Poet and Jean Armour had five sons and three daughters; the latter died in infancy. Three sons reached adulthood; Robert, the eldest, was a distinguished undergraduate at the University of Glasgow and he later had one daughter. William Nicol Burns had no children and the third son, James Glencairn Burns, had a daughter and a son named Robert who died in Chicago. In 1908, the *Burns Chronicle* reprinted a paragraph from the *Glasgow Courier* in 1850, in which it was reported that the Robert Burns murdered off Borneo was a grandson of the Poet and 'Bonny Jean'. However, in 1925, the same periodical claimed that 'the only grandson born to the Bard who bore his full name was a schoolmaster described as Robert Burns the Third, the illegitimate son of the Poet's eldest son. This man died in 1879.[5]

A biography of the poet by James Mackay[6] focused attention on Burns's illegitimate son by Jenny Clow, whom Mackay thought was the father of the young man murdered in Maludu Bay. This grandson boarded at Bellevue House School in Balls Pond Road, Islington or Kingsland, London, which in 1833 was one of thirty-eight such establishments in that district.[7] The Headmaster was a Dutch emigré, Gerrit Van de Linde, who corresponded regularly with the author, Jacob van Lennep, in Holland.[8]

> The school is a secondary modern school of the second class but very respectable, and among the boarders is (mirabile dictu) the grandson of your friend Burns whom I hope to teach as much Dutch as is needed to be able to decipher your translations.

Van de Linde mentioned Burns on several occasions in his letters.

> This morning I counted sixty-one boys in the school, I presently have eleven boarders, among whom one because God willed it is the grandson of your Burns. Send if you can a good wife for me to complete the score.

Later he complained that:

> If I had received what is owed to me I certainly could have done more and on top of that I could have paid off part of my debts in Leyden, but I have been very unfortunate with some boarders. I will probably suffer a loss of thirty pounds from Burns, he has again postponed [paying] until coming October, but I believe I will never receive anything from this pretence ... But that which mainly put me in arrears and disappointed me is a loss of twenty-two pounds which I have suffered from Burns, and twenty-seven pounds which Mr Halton since 1835 ...

An essay entitled *Robert Burns – Explorer of North-West Borneo* published in 1995,[9] referred to an article by Branigan[10] which appeared twenty years earlier in the *Scots Magazine*. This author stated that 'a study of the Burns genealogy will fail to find any mention of a grandson who will fit the facts.' King and Talib drew the same conclusion, while there is no evidence that the Burns of Kayan fame was the grandson of the Bard's liaison with Jenny Clow.

This writer's initial impressions of the explorer were that he was a young man, in his early twenties at most. He lacked Brooke's middle-class background and so important in Victorian Britain, he was without personal fortune and powerful friends. The writer also shared Harrisson's[11] assessment from Burns's papers that Burns was a most interesting and intelligent man with an understanding of native peoples remarkable in his day. He was an astute and accurate observer, fit and able to withstand the physical and mental hardships of an inhospitable environment. Burns, a 'loner', perhaps illegitimate, may have been deprived of affection but imbued with the will to succeed. He was educated as far as could be inferred from his published work and he had an apparent facility with language; he spoke Kayan, some Malay and a little Arabic.

However, the facts presented in this volume were not unearthed in a logical sequence and it was necessary to recast the central character as new evidence came to hand. During this phase of writing it seemed reasonable to explore the possibility that Burns received a university education and the Universities of Aberdeen, Edinburgh, Glasgow, St Andrews and Strathclyde searched their archives. Although a recent foundation, Strathclyde is the repository of the public records of several older institutions of higher learning in Glasgow. Edinburgh,[12] alone, has a Robert Burns in its matriculation indices, he came from Renfrewshire and read medicine in 1820–22. The Faculty of Arts also listed a Robert Burns from Lanarkshire in 1824–25. Faculties of Science did not exist at that time and while the name appeared several times in subsequent class lists, none proceeded to graduation; given their ages, it seemed unlikely that any one was Burns of Borneo.

The Royal Pharmaceutical Society of Great Britain had no record of the man, nor did his name appear in the Medical Directory of 1847 which listed only doctors in England. While it was also unusual, but not unknown, for a Scot to become a Licentiate of the Society of Apothecaries in London, most aspiring medical practitioners obtained their qualifications at a Scottish university. It therefore appeared unlikely that young Burns received a tertiary education, at least in Scotland. Of matriculants of that name, all were too old or had lived beyond 1851, the year of Burns's murder.

The writer's original hypothesis was revised and the view taken that if Robert Burns was a grandson of the Bard, he had descended through an unrecorded extra-marital relationship or that he was unrelated. The association of the Singapore firm of Hamilton, Gray with Buchanan, Hamilton of Glasgow, prompted the thought that Burns might have been employed by the latter before he embarked for South-East Asia, but according to George Nicol, Burns had no prospect of employment when he set foot on Singapore. A search of Buchanan, Hamilton's remaining records in Glasgow's Mitchell Library, revealed no mention of the young man, apart from a reference to him in correspondence between the city's Chamber of Commerce and the Board of Trade. No other archives of Buchanan, Hamilton survive in Glasgow University's Business Centre, nor in the Oriental and India Section of the British Library.

Only two remaining avenues were worthy of exploration. First, a search of British and Singaporean newspapers. The London *Times* of 20 January 1852, reported Burns's murder, adding 'that Mr Burns' incredulity was sincere there can be no question, for though he had been repeatedly warned of the danger he persisted in his voyage without even the precaution of getting up the ship's arms from the hold where they were stored.' Two days later, the *Glasgow Courier* announced under the heading 'Piracy and Slaughter in the Indian Archipelago' that 'Mr Burns, a grandson of the Scotch Poet was dead.' Next day, 23 January, the Glasgow *Herald* quoted from the *Times* 'that Mr Burns, namesake and descendant of the Poet, had died.' Then on Monday morning, 26 January 1852, the day after his alleged grandfather's birthday, the following piece appeared in the *Herald.'*

The Borneo Pirates – The Late Mr Robert Burns

It has been generally stated by the press that this young man, who was recently murdered by the Bornean pirates, was a grandson of the Scottish Bard. He is no relation whatever. The unfortunate Mr Burns was a native of the North of Ireland, and came to Glasgow a few years ago as assistant to his brother-in-law, a respectable draper on the south side of the river. Being of an enterprising disposition, however, he sailed from the Clyde for Singapore in the summer of 1846: and finally formed a connection as a trader in the eastern seas, in which occasion he was employed when murdered by the pirates. His age is about 27.

This statement of Burns's Irish origins and his occupation instigated a search of the Scottish Census for 1841, with particular reference to Glasgow and while several named Robert Burns were found, none fitted the profile of a man born in Ireland in the mid-1820s, but not all the entries were legible. Further searches of Post Office Directories of the period and lists of drapers in the city were of little value in the absence of the name of Burns's brother-in-law. Burns did not appear in the Index to the Merchants House and yet another search of the International Genealogical Index proved fruitless. Short of the impracticable task of scrutinizing the mass of parish registers in Northern Ireland, one possibility remained: Burns's journal. Like Brooke, Burns kept records of daily happenings, but before he left Singapore on his last trading venture aboard the *Dolphin*, he entrusted his journal and the rest of his papers to R. C. Woods,[13] Editor of the *Straits Times*. Sadly they are no longer extant. A second account was found by St John in the *Dolphin's* for'ard cabin after the amok; he passed it to Brooke and it has disappeared. It is not held at Rhodes House, Oxford, nor is it in Admiral B. C. B. Brooke's archive at the National Maritime Museum in Greenwich. The journal is not in the possession of the State Library of Sarawak at Kuching, the Library of the Sarawak Museum, the National Library of Singapore, the National Archives of that republic nor the archives of the *Straits Times*. I reluctantly accepted that it was time to abandon the search.

A brief stopover in Singapore, en route to London and Glasgow in August 1997, provided an opportunity to check the dates of Burns's voyages between his base and Borneo, which were printed in the local press. Issues of the *Straits Times* for 1847 were unavailable in any of Singapore's libraries and the National Library was closed for renovation. So at the suggestion of an unknown librarian in the new town of Tampines, I returned to the National Archives. There were no newspapers, but an entry under 'The Late Robert Burns' was not, as anticipated, an extract from the *Straits Times* of May 1852. It was a letter addressed to the Governor General of British India from M. P . Burns M.D. of 'Origon Territory' in the United States.[14]

No. 690.

From G. Cauper Esquire
Offg. Under Secy. to the Gov.t of India
To the Hon'ble E. Blundell
Offg. Governor of Prince of Wales' Island
Singapore and Malacca.
Dated the 31st August 1853.

Dehart Hon'ble Sir,

I am directed to forward to you the accompanying copy of a letter from Mr. M. P. Burns dated the 5th of May last, and to request that you will communicate to this Department any information you may be able to obtain in respect to the death of his brother Robert Burns, and to the property left by him.

I have the honor to be
Hon'ble Sir,
Your most obedient Servant

Geo. Cauper

Offg. Under Secy. to the Gov.t of India

Williams
31st August
1853.

Letter from the Under Secretary to the Government of British India to the Governor of Prince of Wales' Island, Singapore and Malacca, enclosing a request (opposite page) from Mr M. P. Burns concerning his brother's property.

Opposite: Letter from Matthew Burns M.D. to the Governor General of British India.

136

Oregon Territory Yamhill County
Lafayette May 5 1853.

To The Governor General of British India –

Dear Sir,

By a letter lately received from Glasgow, Scotland, dated February 5 1853. I received the mournful intelligence that my brother Robert Burns a resident of Singapore, was killed on the coast of Borneo by pirates while engaged in trading upon his own vessels. The vessel was afterwards captured by an English Man of War and taken to Singapore. Any information that you can give me relating to his death, and the condition and amount of his Estate will be thankfully received. Direct your communications to me at Lafayette Yamhill County. Oregon Territory via San Francisco California

Remain
Dear Sir
very Resp't. Your
Obedient Servant
so Matthew P. Burns. M.D.

(True Copy)

137

Chapter XVIII

M. P. Burns

On 31 August 1853, G. Couper, the Officiating Under Secretary to the Government of India, wrote to the Governor of Prince of Wales' Island, Singapore and Malacca that he had been directed to forward a copy of a letter from a Mr M. P. Burns and he requested that any information on the death of Robert Burns and the property left by him, be sent to his department. The following reply[1] was sent to Fort William for dispatch to Oregon Territory.

No 94
Sent No. 504
of 1853

The Officiating Under Secretary
to the Government of India
Fort William

dated Singapore 6th October 1853

Sir,

In reply to your letter No. 690 of the 31st August last calling for any information relative to any property left by the late Mr R. Burns; I beg to state for the information of the Most Noble The Governor General of India in Council that the Local Authorities in the Straits, are not aware of the existence of any property while from the enclosed copy of a letter from the Resident Councillor of Singapore, d/15 Sept. 1853 no.165 and its enclosure, it appears that Mr Burns died insolvent.

The depositions alluded to in Mr Church's letter, have been published by order of the House of Commons.

(signed) E. A. Blundell
Officiating Governor

Yamhill County, which Matthew gave as his address, was the second of the four original districts created by the Provisional Legislature of Oregon Territory in 1843. Bounded by the Willamette River in the east to the Pacific coast and from the Yamhill River in the north to the Californian border, its area covered twelve thousand square miles and was named after its original inhabitants, the Yamhill Indians, who were displaced to the Grande Ronde reservation in 1855. The earliest immigrants came to Yamhill in 1814 and most were employed by the various fur companies that operated in Oregon. Some thirty years later, many of the American settlers who followed the Oregon Trail settled in the region, which became the agricultural centre of the Willamette Valley. Lafayette, where Matthew lived, became the county seat in 1847.

It is not known when he arrived in Oregon nor how long he remained in that town. Matthew is not listed in the Census of 1850, and although it may be inferred that he practised medicine, there is no record. The first courthouse, purchased in 1850, was originally a country store in Lafayette and its archives, with the exception of probate and land records, were destroyed when the building was razed in 1857. Burns, spelt Burnes, was declared a tax delinquent in 1853 because of his indebtedness to the Territorial Government for the sum of seven cents.[2] What occasioned his removal north is unknown, although it is possible that he decamped, after issuing a Promissory Note for one hundred dollars to George L. Storey in Portland, Oregon.

Matthew is next heard of in Washington Territory, when 'Mathew P. Burns, late of the County of Pierce aforesaid – Physician', was summoned to appear before a Grand Jury on Thursday, the sixth of November, 1854,[3] on the charge that:

> Being a person of a quarrelsome and turbulent temper and disposition and contriving and intending not only to vex, injure and disquiet one Charles L. Moses and do the said Charles L. Moses some grievous bodily harm but also to provoke instigate and excite the said Charles L. Moses to break the peace and to fight a duel with and against him the said Mathew P. Burns on the 5th day of May A.D. 1854 at the County of Pierce aforesaid wickedly willfully and maliciously did send and deliver and cause to be sent and delivered unto him, the said Charles L. Moses a challenge to fight a duel with and against him the said Mathew P Burns – to the great damage, scandal

and disgrace of the said Charles L. Moses in contempt of the laws, contrary to the form of the statute in such cases made and provided and against the Peace and dignity of the Teritory of Washington.

The Grand Jury found for the Plaintiff but there is no record of the hearing or the judgement.

The doctor was again in trouble with the law in 1855. On 19 July, Burns[4] was called to appear on 5 November at the next term of the District Court to answer a civil complaint brought by Charles W. Swindle for 'a note of hand' for $100, dated Portland 20 June 1853 'whereby the said defendant promised to pay George L. Storey or order, on demand the sum of one hundred dollars ($100.00).' Burns was stated to have refused to pay, in spite of frequent requests by the plaintiff.

1859 was an inauspicious year for Matthew. On 30 September in the District Court of the Second Judicial District of Washington Territory, Charles Morrill of San Francisco[5] was Plaintiff in a civil action against the doctor 'for the sum of $342.85 with interest at the rate of 2% per month from and after July 1st 1859, by reason of a certain draft upon the said Matthew P. Burns.' The debt plus interest was declared in the amount of $372.97 on 18 October, with $24.40 for costs and interest. Burns was then obliged to pay a bill for $399.67 to Freeman and Company in connection with this case and the debt was settled on 6 January 1860.

A few months later, Matthew[6] was again in court as defendant in another civil suit lodged by Miles and Pray of Olympia for non-payment of a Promissory Note issued on 21 March 1859 for $69.87:

The Plaintiffs had sold and delivered a list of articles, liquors and sundries described in an attached bill of particulars annexed to the complaint.

Burns paid $25 on account, 'on or about 13th Jan. 1860'. The amount outstanding, $126.62, was that owed for cigars, whisky, brandy and sundry items.

Although Matthew appears to have been chronically in debt, an official census taken on 19 June 1860, by the Assistant Marshall in Olympia,[7] described him as a male of 32, a surgeon, born in Scotland with real estate valued at $4000 and personal estate of $2000. He was relatively affluent.

He appeared to live alone or with the Ruds, a family of three who hailed from Kentucky.

Examination of the Indirect Index of Thurston County, Washington Territory[8] reveals that Burns bought 160 acres from Isaac H. Clark. On 12 April 1859 he procured 'a city lot' part of Olympia and on 19 April 1860 he acquired from John M. Swan four lots of Block 57 for $210.

The last record of Matthew in Olympia[9] was of confiscation of his land by the Sheriff on 28 April 1863. On that day the Sheriff seized and 'took into execution' the following described real estate, 'there being no personal property belonging to the said defendant to be found':

Lots No. 1, 2 and 3, and part Lot No. 4, in block 57, all being and lying in what is known as Swan's addition to the town of Olympia, Thurston Co. W.T.

Chapter XIX

Matthew Burns M.D.

O n 13 January 1855, the following notice appeared in the *Pioneer and Democrat*, a weekly newspaper published in Washington Territory.

M. P . Burns

Physician and Surgeon

Licentiate of the faculty of Physicians and Surgeons, Glasgow, Scotland; member of the College of Physicians and Surgeons, Canada.

Having had the experience of fourteen years in the profession and practice of

MEDICINE AND SURGERY

in all its various branches in England, India and the United States, and now a resident of Steilacoom, Pierce county, W.T., can be consulted as above

N.B. – A supply of genuine medicine on hand.

Terms moderate.

Jan. 13, 1855 – 3m18

Fort Steilacoom was one of the earliest settlements in Washington Territory and was built in 1849 as a military post of the US Government. The town was incorporated in 1854 and was the headquarters and base of operations for the regular army in the Puget Sound.

One of Matthew's patients was the first person with a psychiatric disorder to attract attention north of the Columbia River. He was Edward Moore, a seaman found wandering on a beach a few miles north of Seattle in 1854. Moore had lived aimlessly for some time, sustained by eating raw mussels and with occasional help from Indians, but becoming progressively more psychotic. The Europeans who found him, placed him in an hotel where he was examined by a Dr Williamson, who found that the patient's toes were frozen. The lack of surgical instruments did not deter the doctor who chose to amputate and he effected ablation with an axe.

Moore's expenses were met by the inhabitants of Seattle and King County for some time, until the patient was transferred to Matthew's care at Steilacoom. The authorities of King County had promised to obtain funds from the Territorial Legislature for continued treatment, but when Matthew presented his account for $1656, payment was declined on the grounds that Moore was not a legal resident. A more compelling reason was probably that the Territory's total income in 1855 was $1199.88. Burns returned his patient to Seattle before the unfortunate man was finally sent to San Francisco where no more was heard of him.

The Governor of Washington Territory was Isaac Stevens and in 1855, in pursuance of his plan to negotiate with the Indians in the region, he spent the summer and autumn travelling through country between the Cascades and Rocky Mountains. But before he could return to Olympia, the territorial capital, the Indians attacked settlers in the Puget Sound area and the entire division was aflame. Stevens was obliged to return through bands of hostile braves and with great skill, he escaped to Olympia in January 1856.

At that time the Indian population in the Northwest exceeded that of the Europeans at least ten-fold. The first whites were explorers or fur hunters not intent upon making a permanent home; they were a source of firearms, powder and other trade goods. Then came the missionaries, seemingly wholly bent on evangelism and not disposed to the acquisition of Indian land. But they were followed by families in trains of wagons that groaned under the weight of ploughs, seeds and all the implements required for permanent settlement. These whites took the choicest hunting-grounds and were often overbearing and arbitrary in their dealings with the Indians, whose resentment grew.

In 1836, Marcus Whitman, a medical missionary, and his wife, Narcissa, came to Oregon Territory with the Reverend Henry and Eliza Spalding to bring Christianity to the Indians. They established their first mission at Waiilatpu, near Walla Walla, among the Cayuse. Whitman was recalled in 1842, when the American Board of Commissioners for Foreign Missions ordered the curtailment of missionary activity, so he journeyed to Boston on horseback to dissuade the Board. Along the way he urged Americans to settle in Oregon. Narcissa and Eliza were the first white women to cross the Rocky Mountains, on what was to become the Oregon Trail and their experiences inspired many others to move westwards. On his return, Marcus helped guide the first large wagon train across the trail in 1843 and the Whitman Mission became an important stopping-point for immigrants until 1847. In that year, deep cultural differences and a measles epidemic, in which many Indians died and which they attributed to sorcery or the Whitmans' God, caused them to kill the missionaries and twelve of their associates.

The frontier remained tense until the Yakima killed several settlers in 1855. Now atop the enormous stresses of pioneer life, the immigrants were obliged to desert their farms, build stockades and seek protection in Steilacoom, Olympia and Vancouver, Washington Territory.

The historian, H. W. Scott,[1] maintained that if all the Indians in the region of the Puget Sound had united, the whites could have been exterminated. However, the tribes on the west side of the Sound and most who inhabited the islands, remained loyal or at least did not join the warring faction.

In the absence of Governor Stevens, Acting Governor Mason, then aged twenty-five, administered the Territory. The only regular army detachment north of Fort Vancouver was about 150 strong and stationed at Fort Steilacoom under the command of a young captain, Maloney. When Major Raines, Maloney's superior at Fort Vancouver, learned of the massacres east of the Cascades he dispatched Major Granville Haller with a force of eighty-four men to punish the Indians, who had broken a treaty of friendship signed only a few months before.

On 27 September, Captain Maloney ordered Lieutenant William Slaughter with about forty men to proceed over Naches Pass and cooperate with Major Haller in punishing the dissident Yakimas. But as Slaughter reached beyond the summit, his scouts informed him that a large force of hostile Indians lay to his front and that Major Haller had suffered a reversal. Slaughter immediately fell back to the White River to await further orders and reinforcements. Haller's engagement with the enemy persuaded the civil and military authorities in Washington and Oregon Territories that war was a reality and Governor Mason called for the raising of two companies of volunteers, including boys above the age of fifteen. Captain Gilmore Hays organised Company B of the First Regiment of Washington Territorial Volunteers at Olympia with about ninety men in addition to commissioned officers. The Company was mustered into service on 14 October 1855 and reported to Captain Maloney on the 20th.

Matthew Patrick Burns volunteered as Surgeon to Company B with the rank of Captain and he appears in the Muster Rolls[2] as:

Surgeon, Age 31, Nativity: Scotland, Height 5'8" Complexion: Fair

Color Hair: Red: Color, Eyes: Blue Residence: Pierce County.

He was inducted on 14 October and was soon to see action.

Maloney left Fort Steilacoom on 21 October to join Lieutenant Slaughter on the White River for an expedition into Yakima country. He then waited until the 24th when Hays arrived with his Volunteers. On 28 October, Maloney rested his force and reviewed his position. He was aware of the folly of advancing into apparent annihilation with two to three thousand Indians in his path, especially with the safety of the Puget Sound territory dependent upon his troops. He also realised that snow would soon cut off his retreat. So he chose to withdraw and sent a dispatch carried by an express rider to his Commanding Officer via Lieutenant Nugent at Fort Steilacoom.

Subsequent events in Pierce County proved the wisdom of Maloney's decision. The settlements east of the Sound were razed. Those who escaped fled to Olympia, Steilacoom and Seattle. According to Scott:

> In the pioneer life of America no more pitiable conditions ever existed. The people were absolutely destitute and the rainy season had opened with unusual violence; but the people of Olympia honored themselves and our common nature by throwing open their homes and sharing all they possessed.

This was not, however, a war between good and evil, the enlightened and the savage. Fearful atrocities were committed by both sides. Burns re-enlisted for a second term and served until September 1856 when a truce was declared.

On 10 April 1857, *The Pioneer and Democrat* carried the following notices:

REMOVED

Dr M. P. Burns, late of Steilacoom, Pierce Co., W.T., has removed to Olympia into the house formerly occupied by John G. Parker, on Main Street, next door to Wilson and Dunlap's new store.
Olympia, April 9th, 1857.
M. P. Burns
PHYSICIAN, SURGEON & OCULIST
OFFICE:

Next door to Wilson and Dunlap's
Main Street, Olympia, W.T.
Dr M. P. Burns returns his sincere thanks for the liberal share of pat-
ronage he has received the past five years from a discerning public.
Dr Burns can be consulted daily at his office, except when absent on
professional business. Those residing at a distance can do so by mail.
A genuine supply of MEDICINES on hand.
NB Particular attention paid to diseases of the Eyes and Chronic
diseases of the Blood.
Olympia, April 9th, 1857   y-no.20

About eighteen months later, Matthew removed to an office in the
new drug store, 'next door to the Pacific House, Main Street, Olympia.'
Not only did he return his grateful thanks for the liberal patronage which
he had received from the citizens of Olympia and the surrounding country,
but he informed them that 'no pains will be spared on his part to serve
faithfully those who may employ him or consult him in his office.'

Dr Burns's expertise now embraced chronic diseases of the Ears, Bladder
and Urethra and he paid particular attention to 'that formidable disease, stric-
ture of the Urethra, and all chronic diseases of the system and blood.'

Consultations on Mondays and Saturday were free from 'eight o'clock,
A.M. to 12M.' He also offered 'Drugs and Patent Medicines, cheaper than
ever sold in Olympia.' More than fifty were listed, among them:

Dr Burns' Solid Extract of Cubebs, Copavis and Sarsaparilla. Dr
Burns' Eye Water, Dr Burns' Ear Wash, Batchelor's Hair Dye,
Suspensary [sic] Bandages – Male, Graefinder Pile ointment and
Thurlington's Balsam of life.

Apart from his continued appearances in civil actions there are few
existing reports of Matthew. He dabbled briefly in politics in 1858 when
he attended a meeting of the Democratic voters of Olympia Precinct whose
aim was the appointment of delegates to the Democratic County
Convention to be held in Olympia on 12 June of that year. Eighteen were
chosen and a further group, that included Matthew, was enrolled.

On 27 May 1859, the *Pioneer and Democrat* published a batch of
accounts for expenses incurred by the Volunteers during the hostilities
which included a bill submitted by Burns. He charged:

... the rent for a hospital for this company up to the 19th of February, 1856, or nineteen days after it was discharged, $400 for the value of two horses and a saddle alleged to have been lost in the service of this company.

Towards the end of the year, Burns moved his office yet again and inserted a fresh card in the local newspaper:

DR. MATTHEW P. BURNS.
OFFICE OPPOSITE THE NEW STAGE OFFICE, MAIN
STREET, OLYMPIA, W. T.
DR. BURNS RETURNS THANKS TO THE CITIZENS of
Washington Territory for the liberal share of public patronage he
has received for the last seven years, while practising Medicine and
Surgery in all their various departments.
Dr. B.'s Surgery is furnished with a complete assortment of
Surgical Instruments, many of them new and patented improve-
ments of eminent Surgeons in Europe.
Dr. Burns respectfully informs his numerous friends that he has
lowered his rate of charges to suit the times. *Calls punctually
attended to night or day.*
Olympia, Dec. 9. 1859.   3y

DR. MATTHEW P. BURNS.
OFFICE OPPOSITE Mr WINDSOR'S STAGE OFFICE, MAIN
STREET, OLYMPIA, W.T.
DR. BURNS, when absent on professional calls, will leave word
when he will return at the office of J. J. Westbrook's Livery Stable,
where he keeps his horse.
Olympia, Dec. 9, 1858.   3y

Matthew's reduced rates for consultations suggest that he was in financial difficulty and the *Washington Standard* of 11 May 1861 advertised a
sale of his land by order of the Sheriff to satisfy a judgement against him.

Sheriff's Sale
By virtue of an order of sale, issued by the clerk of the district court
of the 2d Judicial District of Washington Territory, and to me direct-

ed, I have levied upon, seized, and taken into execution, the following described property, which I shall sell, at public auction, to the highest bidder, at the door of Dr. M. P. Burns' drug store, in Olympia, on Saturday, the 1st day of June, 1861, at the hour of one o'clock in the afternoon ...

The above described property will be sold, or so much thereof as will satisfy a judgement, rendered by the above named court at its March term, 1861, in favor of H. H. Snow, and against M. P. Burns, with interest on the same, and costs.

WILLIAM BILLINGS,
Sheriff of Thurston county, W.Y.
April 27, 1861.   24:4W

A second sale of real estate was authorised on Wednesday, 14 October 1863, to satisfy a judgement, in favour of U. G. Warbass and against M. P. Burns, given in August 1860. But Burns disappeared from ken in 1863 and was probably long gone when the Sheriff called to execute the warrant.

Matthew's subsequent whereabouts are uncertain, but he appears to have fled north. Skilled, sober and reliable physicians were in demand in those days and townships were frequently dependent upon practitioners from distant places. At times, the want was so acute that advertisements in newspapers promised liberal patronage and an excellent income. Military surgeons in the garrisons were reluctant to treat civilians; ten dollars were freely paid for a doctor's call and that sum was also paid to a druggist for a prescription, which in 1904 cost fifty cents.

Matthew became as notorious in the Upper Puget Sound as a Dr Maynard in Seattle.[3] The former was noted for his predilection for surgery, whereas the latter 'was distinguished for his prodigality and fondness for whisky'. Matthew was reputed to be most happy when he had an opportunity to mutilate or dismember a patient, in contrast to Maynard who was wont to worship 'at the shrine of Bacchus'. If Burns was consulted, because of a felon on a finger or a bruise on arm or leg, he invariably recommended amputation. Although he sold healing salves, he viewed them with disdain and he contemned the poultice. It is not surprising that few braved his operating table because of his apparent monomania for amputation. Prosch believed that Maynard was a lesser danger to his patients.

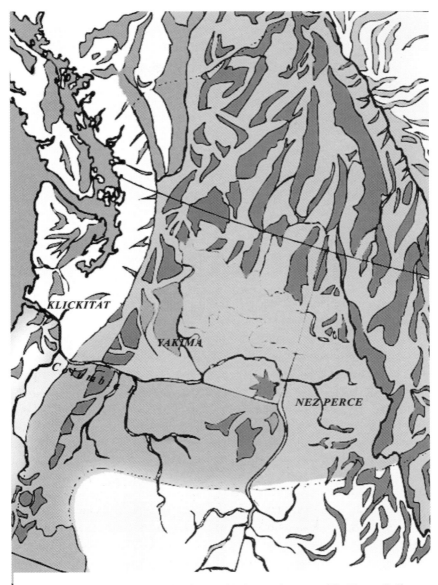

Map of Washington Territory, USA, in the mid-nineteenth century. The Plateau Indians occupied territory between the Cascade Range (nearer the North Pacific Ocean) and the Rocky Mountains. Three of the 36 tribes are shown. The Yakima led the uprising in 1855 with several groups that included the Klickitat. The Nez Percé joined the WT Volunteers as a mounted regiment.

Chapter XX

Matthew Burns – Regimental Surgeon

On 9 October 1855, the *Pioneer and Democrat* stated that:

It now appears to be an established fact that the Yakima Indians, *as a tribe*, have assumed an attitude of open warfare against the United States government and people, and will be dealt with, until terms are made, by our military and civil authorities, as enemies defined in the terms of Indian warfare. Their recent cowardly and cold-blooded murder of Indian Agent Bolon, and some twenty other whites, should act as an incentive to justify no lenity or quarters to be shown to the adult male members of the tribe, by the force sent out against them. We trust they will be *rubbed out — blotted from existence* as a tribe, and that all confederates, aiders and abetters, will be sumarily punished, by being forever quieted. There can be no good result by the adoption of *half-way* measures — the old Levitical law should have free and full force.

After Matthew was commissioned on 14 October 1855,[1] he first served for ninety-three days during which he wrote an inordinately large number of letters to those in authority, notably Governor Stevens and James Tilton, Adjutant-General of the Washington Territorial Volunteers. Burns was Surgeon to Company B with the rank of Captain and he saw action within two weeks of enlistment. On 28 October, he was ordered to join an escort for the express riders, Major William Tidd and John Bradley, who carried dispatches from Captain Maloney to Acting-Governor Mason via Lieutenant Nugent at Fort Steilacoom. Tidd, a carpenter from the English West Country, rode with Bradley and four members of the Volunteers, Lieutenant Colonel Joseph Miles, George Bright, Sheriff Antonio Rabbeson and Dr M. P. Burns. The troop was commanded by A. Benton Moses, a twenty-eight-year-old retired Colonel, veteran of the Mexican War. The account that follows is largely based upon Rabbeson's letter to the press, written on 5 November 1855[2] and the observations of Ezra Meeker,[3,4] a contemporary of Matthew Burns and a member of the jury of Chief Leschi's initial trial for the murder of Colonel Moses.

On the day the horsemen left camp, at the first crossing of the Naches River, Indians slaughtered three families in White River settlement and within twenty-four hours, Lieutenant James McAllister of the Puget Sound Rangers and a Mr Michael Connell were killed near Connell's Prairie, while on a friendly mission to Chief Leschi's camp. Eaton and his cavalry were also besieged for more than four days before they escaped. Meanwhile the express was riding hard for Fort Steilacoom unmolested until mid-afternoon the following day, when the horsemen were off the mountain racing towards Connell's Prairie in the White River valley. Emerging from a patch of woods, they pulled up in astonishment before a party of about one hundred and fifty Klickitat and Nisqually warriors. The Indians appeared not to have anticipated trouble from the east, and had no out-riders in that direction, otherwise the express would have almost certainly been attacked before reaching the plain. Having discovered that Connell's house had recently been burned, Moses asked if the Indians knew anything of the circumstances, but they denied all knowledge and 'declared themselves entirely peaceable — saying that their hearts were right towards the Americans.'

The express spent a long time talking, in an attempt to learn why the Indians were in the area and if their intentions were as amicable as they insisted. The Volunteers then visited a site where they supposed the Indians would set up camp and 'endeavored to purchase some 'mockasins' from their squaws'. There they met and 'conversed awhile' with the great chief, Leschi. Matthew muttered something about 'shooting a few varmints' but he was quickly silenced by Moses, who observed that the warriors had gradually dispersed, so he ordered his men out.

The road westwards from the prairie led through a narrow defile in a swamp, scarcely wide enough for one wagon, with much fallen timber and dense underbrush on each side. Mud and water were very deep for a full three-quarters of a mile and the horses struggled and plunged, their hooves sucking ooze at every step. The ambush was triggered at almost the same spot where McAllister and Connell were cut down four days earlier and where they lay unburied. As the horses floundered through the quagmire in single file, a burst of 'murderous' fire poured out of a tangle of willow and salal (Gaultheria shallon). Moses was struck on the left side of his back, the shot passing immediately under his heart to emerge through his right breast, piercing a letter in his overcoat pocket. The one-ounce balls fired by the Indian muskets caused appalling damage at close range, but Moses contrived to remain in the saddle. Miles, shot through the neck, fell in deep mud with blood pumping from the wound. His companions yelled for him to grab his stirrup-leather and seizing his horse's bridle, whilst spurring their own mounts, they managed to drag him out of the swamp before he lost his grip. All this time, the Indians fired continuously from a range of less than thirty yards. As they rode off, Tidd received three slugs of buck-shot in the head but they failed to penetrate his skull.

A mile and a half from the morass, Moses fell from his horse and was too weak to remount, so the Volunteers carried him some two hundred yards off the trail and wrapped him in their coats, before hiding him in the brush and riding for help. At Fennell's Creek they spotted signs of anoth-er ambush so they dismounted and charged into the undergrowth, two on one side, three on the other, 'Each of us discharging the full contents of our revolvers, and then using our sabres, completely routing the Indians who fled.' But after the skirmish the Volunteers were unable to find their hors-es so they retraced their steps to where they left Moses. He was told what had happened and they promised to return as soon as possible. As they left, the dying man raised himself on one elbow and whispered, 'Boys, if you escape, remember me.'

Leaving Fennell's Creek, they caught sight of a party of Indians on the far side and they ducked into the underbrush, except for the excitable Dr Burns. Muttering, 'The hell with it,' and that he would fight until he died, he waded into the creek, sloshed across and disappeared into a stand of alder. There followed a wild yell, three shots, then silence. The survivors remained hidden until dark, debating whether to try to reach Maloney's force or to head for Steilacoom. Choosing the latter, they floundered on in the dark, at times waist-deep in water or entangled in thickets of under-brush and fallen timber. 'The night was very disagreeable, raining and dark in the forepart of the night and freezing in the afterpart.' When they rest-ed, two lay on the ground with two on top to provide warmth. At other times they blew warm breaths in each other's face. They reached the immi-grant road from Naches Pass about daylight but were afraid to follow it in case they were seen. So the little band struck across country to the Payullup river which they reached about noon, working along the bank in search of a ford. At the edge of Lemon's Prairie they stopped and hid in deep mud and water until long after dark, 'All the while shaking with cold so much our cartridge boxes rattled like cowbells.' Two Indians took cover in the willows overlooking the shallows they had just crossed and while the Volunteers might have easily shot them, they feared that gunfire would attract more. They crept away, 'scraping sticks and leaves from under our feet as we stepped, until out of hearing.'

Once again they reached the immigrant road and with no more rivers to cross and too exhausted to worry about concealment, George Bright staggered into the bracken, collapsed and instantly fell asleep. Unable to rouse him, his companions trudged on until they reached the Tallentire claim on Clover Creek, about three o'clock on Friday morning. Tallentire and a friendly Nisqually hunted until dawn before they located Bright. The survivors reached Fort Steilacoom about two hours before noon and a party of Volunteers was dispatched to recover the bodies of Miles, Moses and Burns. However, when they stopped at the Lemon claim on the Puyallup river to search for fodder for their horses, they found Matthew in the barn hidden in a barley sack.

Unknown to Burns, Lieutenant Nugent[5] sent a dispatch to the Adjutant-General when the surviving members of the express reached camp on 2 November. He informed Tilton that Miles and Burns were dead and that the mortally wounded Moses was left in the woods. After urging Tilton to 'Hurry up the Rangers so that there may be short work of this matter,' Nugent wrote that 'You had better let Mrs Moses know this sad news yourself. If he is still alive Capt. Wallace will rescue him. Yours in haste.'

When Matthew learned of this report, he was incensed at having been given up for dead and at once wrote a complaint to Tilton:[6]

Sir,

Please contradict the report that I was killed by the Indians on Wednesday last. I killed seven with my own hands. They hunted me through the brush for one mile with dogs and lighted sticks, and every one who carried the light I shot. The only wound I got was a skin wound in the forehead from a buckshot. I lived in the brush on leaves and shot an Indian, this morning, for his dried salmon and wheat at Mr Lemmon's. Give my respects to Bright and Rabbeson, and let them know I am safe – only I had to throw away my boots and my feet are badly hurt. Lost my horse, instruments and medicine case. My horse was shot in the kidneys in the swamp where we received a murderous discharge of balls and buckshot. Please let Mr Wily say I am all right.

I remain Respectfully,
M. P . Burnes
Surgeon Capt. Hay's Com.

On 9 November 1855, the *Pioneer and Democrat* published a letter from a Mr Lodge[7] encamped at Connell's Prairie:

The last letter I wrote you was rather a gloomy one, as I was then in anticipation of a forward march. There is every reason now, much more than then, to think that almost everyone of us would have perished by starvation, thirst, fatigue or murder.

The snow on the summit was six inches deep, and the weather cold. It rained during the several days we were coming down the mountains, and I have no doubt that the snow there now is impassable for our train. There was no feed for three days, and we were obliged to give our horses flour. Since the news of Connell's house and barn being burnt, we have been actively on the lookout.

Yesterday morning we reached the burning ruins, and entered into a thorough search of the premises, expecting to find the bones of our comrades and the express-men, or their bodies concealed in the woods. An undershirt, with two bullet holes and two stabs through it, quite bloody, was found, and is supposed to be Joseph Miles'. A bottle belonging to him, and a book, identified as Rabbeson's, was also found. In the evening the body of 1st Lieutenant McAllister, of the Rangers, was found, brought into camp, and today was arranged for transmission to his friends. The Expressman, Wm. Tidd, and Capt. Wallace's command arrived this afternoon. They discovered on the way the body of A. Benton Moses, who died like a man ...

Later in November, Lieutenant Slaughter, in command of fifty regular soldiers and two companies of Volunteers, ordered a halt and at nightfall on the 25th they were attacked by Indians who made off with some horses. During the affray, the animal ridden by Burns on 31 October galloped into camp, caparisoned with saddle, saddlebags, sword and other accoutrements, just as he was when lost by Burns. Indian superstition had probably deterred them from seizing the animal.[4]

On 24 January 1856, Matthew[8] informed the Adjutant-General that he 'had a conversation this morning' with the Governor about his 'appointment as head surgeon to the volenteree force of this part of the Terty' and he requested Tilton's opinion by return. A postscript noted that Burns could supply medicine and everything needed for the expedition.

On 12 February, Matthew[9] wrote to Governor Stevens from Steilacoom stating that he 'had a conversation with Captain Hays' of Company B of the Volunteers who wanted him to go with him again in the capacity of Surgeon. Matthew informed Hays that he (Burns) had spoken with the Governor on the matter and would like to go with the Volunteers if he was appointed Surgeon-in-Chief. Matthew stated that he could supply all medicines and instruments for the whole expedition:

> ... if your Excellency sees fit to appoint me to that important post.
> You will confeare [sic] a favour and it will take me some time to fit
> out if you send me my appointment. I will be ready in eight days.

This letter was quickly followed with a request to Tilton on the 16th[10] to send instructions on how to proceed and to whom he should address his medical reports. He also sought advice on how to supply himself with medicines and equipment, informing Tilton that he would leave Steilacoom the following Sunday for the Volunteers' camp.

Tilton[11] replied enclosing a commission as Surgeon to the Second Regiment of Volunteers and ordered Matthew to:

> ... repair to the Yelm Prairie and enter the discharge of your duties
> as a surgeon at the Block House (Fort Steven) on Barnard's claim.

A postscript noted receipt of Burns's enquiry about medical supplies and the reappointed surgeon was told to furnish them himself or obtain them by requisition from Surgeon Willard at Olympia. Burns was also told to report monthly on the general health of the command.

Matthew[12] acknowledged his commission on 23 February when he was at Fort Montgomery and five days later, he[13] expressed his indignation to Governor Stevens:

> Sir,
>
> When your general orders No. 4 reached me this day on looking over it I find you have placed me in a second rate position and what I think, not what my Commission reads to me (viz) Surgeon of the Second Rgt. of the Vol. Forceses [sic], if I am not the Surgeon of the Second Rgt you will oblige me if you send me my discharge and you will greatly oblige your humble servant.
>
> I remain with Great Respect,
> M. P . Burns.

Matthew[14] sent a similar letter to Stevens on the same day and on 29 February, he complained again to the Adjutant-General.[15]

> Any medical man you send in my place he can have me medicine and outfit as I do not understand the way my commission reads, (Viz) surgeon of the second Regt of WT Vol. and in the general orders it places me a surgeon of the regt. and Dr Willard placed over me which I do not think is fair play as I have been the first with the vol. and has me at a pecunery loss by leaving my practice and if I am not the surgeon of the Regt please send my discharge by the first express and you will oblige your humble servent.

Tilton[16] wrote again on 2 March when he addressed Burns as Surgeon in the 2nd Regiment and Chief Surgeon.

> Your letter of the 29th Feb is rec[d]. You are entirely mistaken in supposing yourself ranked by Dr Willard. The accident of his appearing in gen. orders a line before you implies nothing. You are entirely independent of each other and are both surgeons in the 2nd Regt. and have distinct fields of duty.
> Your field is with the troops and his to primary medicine and medical stores for yourself and the others ... As to what you say about sending out another 'medicine man' that is impracticable for

two reasons viz. 1st there is nobody of your capacity to supply in your place and 2nd it is not possible to accept resignations from officers in the midst of an expedition.

Matthew was placated and he agreed to remain in his post for another month. By March[17] he was in camp on Connell's Prairie and had treated 'twenty-one men of Companies B and C of the centeral batalion, and the Pioneer Company Sapers [sic] and Miners,' for ailments that included 'intermitant fever, inflamation lungs, bleeding from the lungs, gunshot wound in the hand, toothache (extracted), earache (well), cut hand (getting better), inflamation (eyes better), and gunshot wound in the leg (severley).'

The winter of 1855–56 was unusually harsh with heavy rain and much snow. Troops and Volunteers waded chest deep in running ice and water. Major Hays remonstrated with the Governor against the hardships endured by his men. Stevens was inexorable and in consequence, Hays and two fellow officers resigned.

On 24 March Matthew[18] was vexing Tilton:

Be so kind as to define my duty, whither I am to remain in Camp or go along with the Vol. on duty in the field as all my men in the battalion wants me to go with them when they go to fight the Indians while the wounded in the hospital wants me also to attend to them. You wrote me in your last despatch I would here from head Quarters and the oldest commission would take precedence as regard a regemental surgeon.

Tilton[19] replied on the 27th:

In answer I can only say as you are in the Battalion and under the [command] of Major Hays, you will receive instructions relative to your particular field of duty from that officer.

In a second communication written on the same day, Tilton[20] stated that 'you as the oldest surgeon in the Volunteer service rank every other medical officer in the Vol Service.'

There was little respite from Burns's barrage of demands upon his superiors and in an undated letter to Commissary-General Miller,[21] possibly written in March, he listed his requirements.

Sir.

I find it nescessarey for the comfort of my sick and wounded patients in Hospital at present time you will have to send out immedeeatley a medium sized cooking stove with dishes compleat with nine joints of stove pipe and a set of plates spoons knives and two basons or pans to wash the wounds and some whiskey say 30 gall. – 6 yards bleached cotton sheeting – and tobacco for the men, you will heare from James H. Goudy the particulars of the fights. please send me the whiskey and tobacco pipes and a bottle of black pepper – and a light hat to keep the sun from my nose size No.7 1/8- send my letters rom the Stilicoom post office and informe me if the have accepted my resignation – write me by return express rider.

FOR THE HOSPITAL ARTICLES FOR MYSELF DEPART- MENT DO NOT FOR- GET URGENT

Matthew added a postscript:

... when the first wagon leaves for camp send some straw for the wounded men to lay upon and six coarse towels do not send the hat, as Goudy will get it for me, there is some men badly wounded send the whiskey by first chance.

The doctor then wrote to the Acting Quartermaster at Fort Montgomery.[22]

Sir,

I made a question on Genl. (Winlock) Miller for a cooking stove and a full set of furniture with nine feet of stove pipe and plates, knives and spoons for twelve men, also three wash pans to wash the wounds, and six towels, two bottles of sweet oil and a whole piece of bleached sheeting or cotton cloth to dress the wounds and a keg of Sugar House syrup, as the sick cannot eat meat. If it can be got, three or six pounds of patent yeast powder and two pounds of cream tarter.

You can git the above in Steilacoom. Do not fail to send the above articles as there is Eight men in Hospital, six wounded and others sick. Send plenty of straw and grey cotton to make beds with thread and needles by the first teems from your place, as the men in the hospital with wounds cannot lay on the boards without straw and beds.

Burns added to the requisition later that week:

... some whiskey, say thirty galls, also tobacco for the men and pipes, a bottle of black pepper ... and a light hat to keep the sun from my nose size 7 1/8.

A postscript urged:

Send the whiskey by the first chance.

Burns was at Camp Montgomery on 2 April when he wrote to Stevens[23] informing him that he had secured the escort for the wagon from Captain Maxon's Company and that he would be at Fort Hays 'if nothing hapens [sic] on the evening of the third instant'. He mentioned that Dr Albert Eggers preferred to stop at Camp Montgomery and would prescribe any medicine required. Burns concluded with a request for ten days' leave to attend to the urgent needs of his business:

... and all my Enegeries will be directed to your serviseses [sic] afterwards with cherfullnes and thanks, I remain with respects ...

On 18 April, Matthew reported that he had given medicine to thirty-six patients who were well and on duty. Next day, the indefatigable surgeon[24] wrote to the Governor in support of a Mr Murry of Muck, stating that he had attended him 'all last winter for frost bitten feet'. Captain Hays had sent out his Express rider and provided him with horses to visit his patient when he was confined to bed. Matthew asserted that the man would have left his claim and moved into town had his house not been let and that Murry was innocent of the charge of siding with the Indians. He had done all in his power to assist the Volunteers. When he learned that the Nisqually Chief, Quiemuth, was going to join the hostile faction, 'Mrs Murry snatched a fine rifle from him and kept it as the chief was indebted to them fifteen dollars ... ' He concluded that his patient was one of the most respected citizens in the county and that 'some of the most influential men in Thurston can bear testimony of good moral character.' They, believing like Burns in the man's 'innocencey', hoped 'that he would soon be restored to liberty without a stain on his reputation as a true american.'

Matthew[25] harassed Stevens again, less than three weeks later, with the complaint that after visiting Lieutenant Powell of Captain Achilles' company stationed at Muck, he:

> ... was surprised to see about thirty horses turned into his (L.A. Smith's) wheat and oats and the fence rails down ... The wheat and oats will be required and of great service for feed for the Volenteers if the war continues over this summer.

Burns[26] was at Fort McAllister on 29 April when he submitted a report of his battalion's health, beginning:

> I am unwell and am not able to walk along with the Volenteers as the Indians have stolen five horses from me this last month, and left me without a single horse, therefore I am not able for the duty, on that account, so you will oblige me if you accept my resegnation and releive [sic] me from duty, by the first Express and if I find my horses; and the service requires my serviceses [sic], I will be proud to assest the Troopes [sic] if I am required ...

A second letter[27] was sent to Tilton on the same day with Matthew's account of the sick and wounded, including his amputation of a finger accidentally injured by a gunshot. He concluded that:

> ... since I moved the Hospital here I have no house and no accomadation. I have written to Gov Stevens to send my resignation by next Express – as I am sick from cold and fatigue from walking and cold.

Stevens graciously acknowledged Burns's communication concerning the forage and referred the matter to Lieutenant Colonel Shaw for action. Then on 1 May 1856, Tilton[28] formally accepted Burns's resignation as Surgeon in the Second Regiment with effect from the arrival of his successor. Three weeks later, Matthew[29] wrote to his Commanding Officer, Colonel Shaw:

> You will send ten men of the Right Winge [sic] of the 2nd Rgt W T

Vol to escort M. P . Burns Surgeon Centreral Battalion to [illegible] patients of the above Regiment ...

One might suspect that Matthew was somewhat unaware of military protocol or that his relationship with Shaw was less than amicable, because Shaw accused Burns 'of the military crime of endeavouring to create disaffection to the Commander in Chief', in a report to the Adjutant General and placed Burns under arrest.

Tilton[30] wrote that he approved of Shaw's action in a letter dated, 21 May, and stated that:

> You will confer with him, point out the inevitable consequences to the detriment of the service of such a course, and advise him to retract and promise to be more guarded in future, in the expression of any feelings of disapprobation he may entertain.
>
> Should this officer accede to this proposition, relieve him from arrest. Should, however, he refuse, you will cause a charge of 'endeavouring to cause mutiny' to be prepared, set forth the specification of time, place, and the words used and place Surgeon Burns upon his trial before the Military Commission on 'General Court Martial' now in session at Camp Montgomery and of which Lt. Col. Hurd is President.'

Eight days later, Tilton[31] wrote to Major Maxon enclosing a blank discharge which he was told to complete and send to Burns, if the latter refused orders to join his company.

> 'Should he never have received such orders, send such to him now and if he refuses – then send him the discharge and mark upon your Muster Roll the date and cause of his discharge.'

On Independence Day 1856, the *Pioneer and Democrat* published the following letter written by Matthew concerning his arrest:

From the Oregon Weekly Times.

'Right Wrongs No Man.'

FORT MONTGOMERY, W.T.,
June 11, 1856.

EDITOR OREGON TIMES — *Dear Sir:* In a number of the 'Oregonian' of May 31st, under the head of 'Indian Troubles in Washington Territory,' and signed 'True Facts.' I read a statement saying that I was arrested by Gov. Stevens for seditious language, &c. In justice to the Governor, and to myself also, I must say that part of the communication is *false*, and the person who caused its publication *knew it to be so*. It is evident that it was done out of feelings of malice, and a desire to do Governor Stevens an injury, and to lead the public mind astray to the best interests of our Territory.

I believe the *entire* communication to be *false*, and to have come from the lips of a foul slanderer.

I am, sir, very respectfully,

M. P . BURNS, M.D.

After resolving some of the problems with the Indians west of the Cascades, Governor Stevens sent a battalion of Washington Volunteers, under Lt Colonel Shaw, east of the mountains to reinforce the volunteers and soldiers in Oregon. They crossed by way of Naches Pass early in June 1856 and marched to Walla Walla, from where they continued to the Columbia river. Matthew appears to have reconsidered his position, because he accompanied the expedition and submitted his monthly report from camp on Mill Creek on 12 July 1856[32] He treated forty-five patients in the Second Regiment:

'Dysentery, 25; congestion of lungs, 2; venereal, 12; inflamation of eyes, 3; blown up by powder, 2 (on the 4th of July, Wright and John Hays, Company K); inflamation of the lungs, 2.'

He looked askance at the Oregon Volunteers and reported that intermittent fever had appeared since their arrival. He concluded his account by noting that:

In a former letter you wrote me when the Regt. would come together you would let me know who was to be Surgeon of the Regiment. Please write me by next Express as my period of service for six months ends in July.

It is possible that Matthew was not the only 'mutinous' member of his Battalion because of a note[33] to Colonel Shaw on 12 July which read:

Our Captain was arrested our Lieut. refused to take command. We have always been and are now ready to perform all lawful duties required of us by the legal Volunteer Authorities
From Company
W. M. Rifles'

Meanwhile, Colonel Shaw had dispatched seventy-five men to coop-erate with the Oregon Volunteers and they succeeded in capturing so many horses and supplies that a large number of Indians were compelled to seek the protection of the Warm Springs reservation. In accordance with Governor Stevens' orders to 'spare no exertion to reduce to unconditional submission any hostiles within reach', Shaw determined to attack an Indian force camped in the valley of the Grande Ronde and he pushed rap-idly over the mountains to engage the enemy.

Shaw[34] reported that:

We arrived in the Grand Ronde valley on the evening of the 16th and camped on a branch of the Grande Ronde river in the timber send-ing spies in advance.

On the morning of the 17th, Shaw rode out with Major Maxon, Michael Marchmean, Captain John and Dr Burns to reconnoitre the area and:

After proceeding about five miles we ascended a knoll in the valley, from which we discovered dust rising along the timber of the river.

Shaw immediately ordered Maxon and John to investigate while he returned to increase the pace of his command.

The troops were instantly formed in order and moved quietly to with-in half-a-mile of the Indian village, when they discovered that the pack train, which had moved to the left, down the Grande Ronde river. Shaw observed:

At this moment a large body of warriors came forward singing and whooping, and one of them waving a white man's scalp on a pole. One of them signified a desire to speak, whereupon I sent Captain John to meet him, and formed the command in line of battle. When Captain John came up to the Indians they cried out to one another to shoot him, whereupon he retreated to the command and I ordered the four companies to charge.

The Indians apparently planned to draw the Volunteers into the brush along the river where they would have had the advantage, but Shaw ordered his men to charge down the river towards the pack train, which split the enemy who were put to flight. Six Volunteers were killed and five wounded and Matthew[35] was reported to have captured:

> ... two squaws and a packed horse with 65 trading musket balls, one and a half pounds of fine rifle powder and English powder horn, one large rigid Allen's revolver loaded and various other items including two white men's scalps, one with grey hairs, the other light colored.

Shaw learned from the prisoners that about three hundred warriors from the Cayuse, Walla Walla, Umtilla and other tribes had taken part.

> The enemy was run on the gallop fifteen miles, and most of those who fell were shot with a revolver. It is impossible to state how many of the enemy were killed ... we may safely conclude that at least forty of the enemy were slain and many went off wounded. When we left the valley there was not an Indian in it and all signs went to show that they had gone a great distance from it.

Matthew was at Headquarters on Camp Mill Creek on 24 July when he wrote to Captain A.H. Robie:[36]

Sir,

You will oblige Dr. M. P . Burns if you bring him the following articles ten gallons good whiskey a pair boots strong No 9 — 1 pair strong pants two wollen [sic] shirts grey = a pair leather gloves = a good riding saddle and bridle = one broad brimed [sic] hat to turn rain (two tooth brushes and comb and one Farenhiats thromometere [sic], all partially deleted) 1 Nevey Revolver and belt 1 neck handkerchief.

A week later, he sent a request to Governor Stevens seeking approval to supply medicines to Lieutenant Colonel Craig for his Nez Percé Mounted Volunteers, led by their War Chief, Spotted Eagle. Craig, a European adopted by the tribe, played a major role in maintaining good relations with the Native Americans. Matthew[37] informed Stevens that:

> ... the flux and dysentery is proving very fatal this season among the Indians and even his own [Craig's] family attacked with it but all are well at present.

Two weeks later, Burns[38] recommended to Shaw, his Commanding Officer, that:

> Captain Joseph and Columbus White be discharged from the service owing to sickness contracted in the service and from the Effects of the Climate not agreeing with theire [sic] Constitution.

Dr Burns's final report[39] tells of forty-two patients treated in the month ending 8 August 1856, and it concludes:

> Private Joseph Stutsull, Company D, who was aceccidentially shot in the thigh in three different places from the discharge of a musket loaded with three balls, died on the 7th inst.

Matthew was still in camp at Walla Walla in September when he informed Stevens,[40] as Governor and Superintendent of Indian Affairs, that Olwhi, the Yakima Chief and another, wished to speak with the Governor in the hope of securing provisions for their people.

> Then he will go away with a good heart he would like to know by return I referred him to you but he wants me to speak for him, he is asking me about his daughter Mrs Edgar.

Governor Stevens strove to preserve good relations with the Nez Percé and he believed that Shaw's victory and the holding of Walla Walla

Valley were important in this regard. A truce was declared and Burns returned to private practice, but peace did not return to the region until 1858, after heated exchanges between the civil and military authorities and the Native Americans, which culminated in their decisive defeat on the Plains of Spokane.

There are few further reports of Matthew apart from his encounters with the law, but on 22 May 1857,[41] he amputated a leg 'affected by a scrofulous disease of the bones forming the knee joint'. Burns was assisted by Drs Willard, Lansdale and Glenn who administered the chloroform.

> The disease was of fifteen years' standing and for the last two years was attended with excruciating pain, and had, during the latter period, confined the patient to the bed. The disease, had it been permitted to take its course, which we are informed could not otherwise have been arrested, would undoubtedly have resulted in death.
>
> The amputation was performed on the upper third of the thigh, and by it full one sixth of the entire human system (22 pounds) was removed. That such can be done without impairing the mental or physical faculties, except so far as the removed limb itself is concerned, would almost seem to be preposterous. Yet such does appear to be the case, and under the care and direction of a skillful surgeon, is attended with comparatively little danger. The time consumed in the operation was but about twelve minutes. The patient is fast convalescing, and will be able, with the use of crutches, to go about in a few weeks.

Matthew's last reported patient was a son[42] of Mr Levi Shelton of The Yelm Prairie:

> While engaged in drawing a cover over a yeager to protect it from the rain, preparatory to a hunt for game, accidentally shot himself through the palm of the hand, thereby most shockingly mutilating that limb.
>
> Upon surgical examination, it was discovered that all the fingers of that hand had been rendered useless, and amputation, above the wrist, had to be resorted to, to save not only the arm, but probably the patient. This operation was ably performed by Dr Burns, of this place, assisted by Drs Willard, Kiser and Glenn of Oregon, while the patient was under the influence of chloroform. The invalid is now doing as well as could be expected.

Chapter XXI

'Who can be ... temperate and furious ... in a moment? No man.'

U ntil the late 1840s, voyages from Britain, such as those made by Nicol, Brooke and Burns, took four to five months. At that time, dispatch of a letter and receipt of a reply within nine months was the acme of punctuality. Most European correspondence arrived via Batavia in the former Dutch East Indies and it is remarkable how families, government and trade survived the constraints of such tardy communication. However, residents of Singapore had to wait until 1845 for more rapid transport. In that year, the Peninsular and Oriental Company introduced its first mail-carrying paddle-steamer, the *Lady Mary Wood* [1] which delivered the London post in forty-one days. Three years on, further improvement occurred locally with the erection of a flagstaff on Government Hill (now Fort Canning) and the wearing of a signal that betokened a ship to the East. The unfurling of the Red Ensign indicated the approach of the steamer with mail from or to Europe, whereas that from or destined for China was signalled by a yellow flag. The latter caused considerable consternation when it was first spied at the masthead, and rumour swept the town that plague had erupted aboard an Arab dhow that transported pilgrims to and from Mecca. [2]

Young Robert Burns probably bade farewell to family and friends in a tumult of apprehension, excitement and sadness which may have given way to terror, as his little ship pitched and rolled through tempestuous seas and black tropical squalls that obliterated light. But once the craft was moored and Burns quit its confines to breathe the sensuous air, dense with the fragrance of frangipani and spices from the bazaar, he would have been enthralled.

In Singapore, Burns met Nicol, a God-fearing Scot who also deferred to Mammon. Nicol was eighteen in 1832 when he arrived to establish Hamilton, Gray and Company with Ellis Gilman. He was undoubtedly kind to Robbie and manifested a fraternal, at times paternal, interest in his welfare. Despite advice to the contrary, he appointed the young man as an agent to the company. It is not known if Burns claimed to be a grandson of the Bard to ingratiate himself in the community or whether it was an assumption made by the press, but the former seems unlikely. A few questions from an astute Scot, like Nicol, would have immediately unmasked an impostor. However, notwithstanding his imperfections, Robbie was an honest man.

In contrast, Nicol appears generally to have hedged his bets, either with his Deity through the Kirk or in his commercial transactions; profit was his goal. One senses that he 'knew his place' and while prominent in Singaporean society, he recognised Brooke's power, rank and ability to make or break in the region. Nicol would have never deliberately placed himself or his company at risk, except on one occasion when he succumbed to 'nutmeg mania' and planted eight thousand trees on his property which quickly became diseased and died.[3] Nicol lost heavily on the venture. One pictures him at ease in the pews of the unco-guid, wearing a benevolent if sanctimonious smile. But despite his parsimony, it is unlikely that Burns would have reached Borneo without his support.

Six months after the *Dolphin* massacre, Nicol wrote to Brooke from Shanghai,[4] informing him that he had received an Edinburgh newspaper in which the Editor 'made some strictures not very complimentary' to Brooke and as the latter had requested Nicol's assessment of the charges laid against him by Burns, Nicol was glad to comment. Another reason for his enthusiasm was that he wished to vindicate himself, as the article made it appear that Nicol 'was concurrent in Mr Burns' proceedings and shared his opinions.'

Nicol continued:

The firm to which he [the Editor] alludes is mine, Hamilton Gray and Co. Mr Burns was recommended to my notice as an enterprising young countryman deserving of support, and as much to assist him as anything else, I agreed to advance him the necessary funds to enable him to obtain a lease of the Bintulu mines, of the great value of which he was very sanguine.

However, it is surprising that despite Nicol's years in the region, his correspondence with Burns reveals considerable lack of knowledge of Borneo, its peoples, products and its dangers.

The lease was obtained, as you are aware, but as it soon appeared that the Sultan was playing false, and that Mr Burns' violent conduct and ungovernable temper were likely to lead to embarrassing results, and as by this time it was quite obvious that the speculation was a bad one, in fact a mere delusion, I made up my mind to have nothing more to do with it or Mr Burns, and declined to have any further connexion with it. In consequence of this, Mr Burns, on his return to Brune, cancelled the bargain with the Sultan and obtained a refund of part of the advances (which were honourably repaid to my firm), though not without, as it afterwards appeared, having recourse to personal threats towards the Sultan, which, but for the awe the latter stood in of British authority, would probably have ended in Mr Burns' life being taken on the spot.

In terminating his dealings with Burns, Nicol declared that he would have willingly helped him to seek his fortune except that he:

... was apprehensive of the consequences his violent temper and reckless disregard of prudence would lead him into. His fate, poor fellow, was a sad and melancholy one, but it did not surprise me, and he was often warned that such a catastrophe would be the result of his overweening confidence in himself.

Nicol informed Brooke that his agent frequently affirmed that he was prevented from working the antimony mines because of Brooke's influence, but Nicol never discovered the grounds for this allegation and subsequent events proved that the assertion was false: Nicol wrote:

On the contrary ... I am firmly persuaded that so far from wishing to place obstacles in our way, you would willingly have assisted in promoting it as far as lay in your power – such was the impression left on my mind by the conversations I had with you on the subject. That you were anxious afterwards to get Mr Burns out of the country, is, I believe, true, for the very sufficient reason that his proceedings, if not restrained, were likely to involve you with the native chiefs. This, I believe, was your true motive for opposing Mr Burns, if a desire to protect his life from the certain consequences he was incurring by the career he was pursuing can be so termed.

Nicol greatly regretted this explanation:

... as it will not create impressions favourable to poor Burns' memory; but justice to the living renders it unavoidable. He was indeed ill advised to appear before the public in this matter, and I cannot but come to the conclusion, that he has been used as a shield under cover of which certain parties might continue their assaults upon you, though in this, as in previous instances, the attempt will recoil with damaging effect upon themselves.

Later, in May 1852, Nicol wrote to the Editor of the *Singapore Free Press*, noting that the Editor of the *Straits Times*:

... still affects incredulity on the subject of the denial of the charges against Sir James Brooke which appeared in your last issue.

He enclosed four letters from Burns, 'all I ever received from him' and dismissed:

... the absurd charge of Sir James Brooke having obstructed my Firm, or their employee Mr Burns, in their private undertakings, or attempted to intimidate me.

Nicol was also most emphatic in his refutation of the report that Brooke had tried to force Burns out of the Bintulu region, citing his agent's letter of 14 September 1848 in evidence. But this date is erroneous and Nicol and/or the *Free Press* must presumably refer to his agent's letter from Labuan of 5 November. According to Nicol, had Burns been compelled to leave Kayan country or had he been threatened with deportation, he would have informed Nicol at the time, or after his return to Singapore. Nicol insisted that he first learned of the matter during a visit to Shanghai, when Brooke wrote to ask if the report was consistent with Nicol's knowledge of the facts.

Nicol continued angrily:

I *now* learn for the *first* time that during Mr Burns' stay in Bintulu a letter was received by the Chiefs from the Sarawak Authorities threatening them with punishment if they allowed him (Mr Burns) to reside there or work the mines.

Nicol was dumbfounded; it was most extraordinary that:

Mr Burns, the employee of my firm, and in charge of their interests, should have preserved towards them and me a complete silence – both in correspondence and personally on this to them most important point, for he could not have been ignorant that it would have been my business – supposing I intended, as I then did, to prosecute the undertaking – to investigate a matter that threatened its success. The affair is inexplicable on any other ground than that the existence of such a letter is fabulous or that its substance has been perverted.

In either case it places Mr Burns' character, I regret to say, in a most unfavourable light. It convicts him either of neglect of duty to his employers and duplicity to them or the still more grave charge of falsehood. I hope for the sake of his own reputation that he has only been guilty of the minor offence.

Nicol claimed that Burns's letter of 5 November 1848 provided conclusive evidence that the young man had been well received by Brooke, the meeting was more agreeable than Burns expected and the Raja had 'kindly offered his assistance as far as in his power.' Burns never expressed a contrary opinion to Nicol on the subject, although 'their intercourse soon afterwards ceased' later that month when the Bintulu venture was abandoned. Nicol was 'heartily sick' of the undertaking and of Burns's 'extravagant delusions about Borneo' and he canvassed the view that Burns's sentiments may have afterwards undergone a change and that:

... he may have reverted to his original morbid and groundless suspicions of Sir James Brooke, out of which I frequently attempted to reason him.

Nicol would have been relieved and pleased if he had been able to find 'some extenuating or justificatory circumstances' for Burns's conduct.

After all, it was he who helped Burns and provided financial assistance, 'and ... in this friendly endeavour I have been a pecuniary sufferer.' Nicol was therefore forced to the painful conclusion that Burns:

> ... had proved himself undeserving of the efforts made on his behalf and that he has justly exposed his character to the charge of ingratitude.

The letter ends with an attack on R. C. Woods, Editor of the *Straits Times*, a staunch supporter of Burns and implacable foe of Brooke.

> My resorting to the columns of a Public Journal on a personal matter has been forced on me unwillingly by the unwarrantable manner in which the name of my Firm has been coupled by the *Straits Times* with that of Sir James Brooke, and as it is in my power to refute the calumny against the latter – a Public servant of high position – I cheerfully break the silence which I would have maintained, had I alone been the object of this unprovoked attack. The Editor mysteriously alludes to certain Correspondence of mine in his possession and resorts to something like a threat that use may be made of it – let me assure him (*altho' he knows it well*) that he cannot do Sir James Brooke or myself a greater service than by publishing ALL* my letters to Mr Burns in his possession. I call on him to do so, and if he declines I leave it to you to publish them if you think fit, for which purpose I now place them at your disposal.
> *I will be satisfied with nothing less than the *whole* Correspondence, – no garbled Extracts.

The *Straits Times* responded four days later, mocking 'the intemperate tone, the bluster and the utter weakness of the production'. The Editor was quite content to leave the matter to the judgement of his readers and the public, but Nicol's unwarrantable aspersions on the memory of 'the individual we are endeavouring to defend' made it a duty to expose the baselessness of those charges. In countering each of Nicol's assertions, the *Straits Times* stated that they had been authorised by a former Master of the *Royalist* who had been shown instructions given to Lieutenant Gordon of that ship, that if Burns could not be prevailed upon by fair means, he was to be forced out of Bintulu.

The first instance of Burns's capricious temper was reported from Brunei where he had gone to request permission to travel to Bintulu. In his initial letter to Nicol in February 1848,[5] he vented his annoyance, frustration and impatience induced by days of procrastination at the Sultan's court. Unknown to Nicol at that time, Burns not only abused the Sultan and his Pangerans in public, but he failed to extend the customary expressions of respect which are integral to Malay society and of which he was probably unaware. In contrast, his behaviour towards the Kayan, during his first lengthy foray into their territory, was exemplary. Gliddon, a rival in the prospective trade, wrote well of him and the Kayan in his letter to Joseph Hume. Moreover, the fact that Burns lived among 'a wild, warlike race' for several months and was allegedly permitted to marry a Chief's daughter, attests to his courage and as Harrisson[6] observed, indicated his rare ability to mix with indigenous peoples. William Napier, the erstwhile Lieutenant-Governor of Labuan, who was suspended and ultimately removed from the Public Service by Brooke, was also complimentary, while noting Burns's warmth of temper. However, Burns was aware of his lack of social graces as he stated in his letter to Palmerston and this, with his apparent tactlessness, most probably reflected his 'class' and poverty of education.

Irwin[7] wrote that it was 'difficult to form a just estimate' of Burns's character, but the quality of his writing showed that he was far from being the 'disreputable adventurer' of Sarawak history. He, too, remarked that Burns had lived for some time among the Kayan which argues that he can hardly have been as tactless and overbearing as has sometimes been suggested. On the other hand he undoubtedly had a fiery temper, and was 'crude and predatory (particularly where women were concerned)' but this statement is hyperbolical and unjust. The only testimony in support of this latter allegation is contained in the letter from 'The Rajahs of Barram to Mr Scott and Mr Low.'

More than one hundred years after receipt of this correspondence in Labuan, Harrisson wrote that it:

> ... hardly bears examination as a serious piece of evidence ... It is addressed in *Malay*, and with a Mohammedan date, to Mr Scott and Mr Low at Labuan, and 'signed' rather grandiloquently by 'three Rajahs of Baram.' No Kayan or others could then read or write and

to this day (1951) they have no idea of the Malay calendar. The letter bears all the marks of being engineered by Brunei Malays, who until then had held a trading monopoly on the Baram and must have been especially upset by Burns arrival – as he himself notes.

Indeed, Burns had written:

That we have heard so much of the imputed horrors of head-hunting and still know so little of the people of the interior of Borneo, might be accounted for by their having been maligned by foreigners, by the atrocious Malays of the coast, who have described them as being savage head-hunters and cannibals ... The object of the Malays is obvious, as they mainly derive their subsistence by cozening the people of the interior of their industriously collected produce, and know that were Europeans to have intercourse with the interior their trade would decline ...

Harrisson noted that Brooke replied to the letter in person without knowledge of the existence of the three 'Rajahs' and with the assumption that Burns was guilty of all charges. And this was from a man, who at that time had no authority or claim to authority on the Baram. Burns was silent, he made no remonstrance, nor did he reply to 'a friend to the absent', the anonymous and somewhat intemperate correspondent who remarked upon his first paper in the *Journal of the Indian Archipelago*.

Harrisson concluded that Burns's 'initial balanced judgements and fairly temperate attitude' which are revealed in his first paper on the Kayan, were probably distorted later by the frustration of his plans and by protracted periods of discomfort, illness and insecurity in dangerous and inhospitable environments.

As a long-term resident of Sarawak with a profound knowledge of its geography, history and ethnology, Harrisson was uniquely able to assess the 'island paradise' and the proximity of death that stalked all in the early days of exploration, particularly by ingenuous, uninformed Europeans such as Burns. However, even with our paucity of information, his murder was especially tragic, because it deprived society of an ambitious, courageous and intelligent young man. Despite his desire to leave his adoptive home in Glasgow, the prospect of committing himself to the unknown must have been daunting at times. Whilst at sea, periods of exhilaration would have been supplanted by terror, in the teeth of sudden storms that cause the heart to race, in the awareness that at any instant, the vessel could have been overwhelmed, shattered and lost forever.

While it is possible, although unlikely, that he pretended to be a grandson of the Bard, he may have assumed the relationship as insulation against the barbs, glances and scorn with which some 'superior' beings despise the less fortunate. Too much emphasis has been laid on Burns's shortcomings with scant heed paid to his achievements as an explorer and ethnographer. Athough Nicol freqently complained that his agent was 'too sanguine' in respect of his prospective antimony trade, had Burns lived he might now be universally remembered as 'Burns of Borneo'.

Chapter XXII

'You shall seek all day ere you find them.'

The discovery of a letter from a sibling appeared to open a more rewarding route to Burns's antecedents and it was thought that a family of at least two brothers, Robert and Matthew, and a sister married to a Glasgow draper would be easier to trace than a singleton. But deducing the genealogy posed several insurmountable difficulties. There are no official registers of births and deaths in Ireland before 1864[1] and inspection of parish registers before that date could not be undertaken.

Matthew was instantly perplexing. In his letter to the Governor-General of India, he signed himself M. P . Burns, M.D. and in 1855, when he published a professional card in the *Pioneer and Democrat*, he claimed to be a Licentiate of the Royal Faculty of Physicians and Surgeons, Glasgow, and a member of the Canadian College of Physicians. But this man is not mentioned in the Register of Licentiates of the Royal Faculty (now College) of Physicians and Surgeons of Glasgow.[2] Furthermore, the Royal College of Physicians and Surgeons of Canada was not founded until 1929, and although he may have been associated with one of the provincial or territorial medical colleges in that country, no record was found.

Burns cited fourteen years' experience in England, India and the United States which was impossible, given that his stated age was thirty-one, when he volunteered for military service in October 1855, thus implying that he completed his medical training at about sixteen years of age. Further correspondence with the Scottish universities revealed no medical graduates of that name in any of Edinburgh's matriculation indices and none in the list of Licentiates of the Royal College of Surgeons of that city.[3] St Andrews University[4] checked for a first degree in Arts and also for the degree of Doctor of Medicine, but found no trace of Matthew Burns.

A Matthew P. Burns attended the University of Glasgow in 1828.[5] He was born in the Barony of Glasgow and studied anatomy, practice of medicine, midwifery, surgery, mathematics, Infirmary Clinical Surgery and PRID (most likely, Post-Graduate Registration in Infectious Diseases). This Burns does not appear in the Matriculation Album of the University of Glasgow, 1728–1858, but matriculation was not compulsory until 1859 and there is no entry in the records of Anderson College of Medicine. Again, the University of Strathclyde[6] found no M. P . Burns between 1820 and 1853. Similarly, his name does not appear in the Roll of Graduates of King's and Marischal Colleges at Aberdeen,[7] nor in any of the English, Irish, Scottish and United States medical directories published in the nineteenth century.

Mr Stephen Greenberg[8] of the History of Medicine Division at the National Library of Medicine, The National Institutes of Health, Bethesda, Maryland, also found;

> ... no mention of Matthew Burns in Lafayette, Yamhill County, Oregon or elsewhere, in any of the Library's directories or biographical dictionaries.

It is possible that Burns attended classes in medicine but did not sit the examination, a common occurrence in nineteenth century Scotland[9] and the reluctant conclusion is that he practised fraudulently. This situation prevailed particularly in the United States and Canada, where some areas, for example, Washington Territory, did not require a licence.[2,10] Perhaps Burns, like Joseph Hume, served as a surgeon's apprentice gaining a knowledge of surgery first-hand. Amputation was a relatively common surgical procedure in Burns's day and an intelligent person could have acquired the necessary skills with teaching and practice. But Matthew's notorious predilection for ablation as a form of treatment, suggests a gross deficiency of clinical judgement. However, he may have served in the army, possibly in India, as speculated earlier, where he could have acquired rudimentary training as a surgeon's assistant, equestrian skills and the ability to handle a revolver, the last two of which may have determined his inclusion in the escort for the express riders. Hard riding in unbroken country is no pursuit for a tiro. But as far as India is concerned, there is no record of him in the Honourable Company's Register of Medical Officers.[11,12]

Attempts to adumbrate the Burns boys were continually balked by the random discovery of new facts, particularly in the case of Robert, and the initial view that both had probably attended university was subsequently negated. The disclosure of Robert's correspondence with Nicol revealed several lapses in grammar eschewed by most Scots of even modest education; for example, 'I had went,' 'I done nothing further.' What remains of Robert's subsequent writings contains no such errors, but his papers in the

Journal of the Indian Archipelago were edited and while one cannot fault his letter to Palmerston in 1851, it is possible that he received assistance, perhaps from Motley or Woods, Editor of the *Straits Times*.

Brother Matthew was, however, an unbridled rogue. He appeared to have been a chronic debtor, who probably fled to Washington Territory from Oregon, after issuing at least one promissory note. Moreover, it was likely that he faced professional competition, with increasing settlement of the Territory and the advent of qualified physicians and surgeons from reputable medical schools. However, his impecuniosity is at odds with his apparent wealth, which was published in the Census of Thurston County in 1860.[13] On that occasion he held real estate to the value of $4000 and his personal estate was given as $2000. It seems unlikely that this small fortune was acquired by diligent medical practice in Washington Territory, and it is possible that Burns saw an opportunity to supplement his income, when he enlisted as a surgeon in the Volunteers in October 1855.

The Bounty Land Law was published in the *Pioneer and Democrat* on 26 May 1855. Every soldier, teamster or other person who saw service in any war since 1790, was to receive a warrant for 160 acres of land, except those, who under other legislation, received that amount.

> This is a most magnificent grant. Millions of acres will be taken under it and in the main, by those who deserve it.

It was estimated that a total of 285,000 applications would be made for the division of 35,800,000 acres and that these would pour into the Pensions Office in overwhelming numbers.

Later, in September, a Special Notice appeared in the local newspaper for the attention of:

> Army Officers, Soldiers, Volunteers, Teamsters, Naval Officers, Seamen, Mariners and Navy Clerks, and their surviving widows and minor children. You are now entitled to a Land Warrant for 160 acres: and if you have already received 40 or 80 acres, you are entitled to an additional quantity, equal to 160 acres. Whether you desire to sell or locate your warrants, it is important that the same be procured without delay, as the great number of warrants which will be thrown upon the market, must soon materially reduce their value.

Applicants were urged to apply to a New York office without delay.

While Burns would have been entitled to a grant of 160 acres, there is no record of it.

In the Muster Rolls of the Washington Territorial Volunteers,[14] Matthew Burns's 'nativity' is given as 'Scotland', but in an address by Mr Harvey Scott,[15] on 3 March 1903, at the Semicentennial Celebration of Washington Territory at Olympia, Burns was described as 'a most eccentric Irishman'. In a footnote, the compiler, Leslie Scott, quoted one of Burns's contemporaries who remembered him:

> ... as an eccentric character, red-headed, choleric, and one who knew
> Latin and French and was interested in botany. I have heard him say
> he was distantly related to the poet, Burns. He extracted teeth with a
> tourniquet, without regard for the feelings of his patients.

Ezra Meeker,[16] another coeval, viewed Burns as a braggart 'who, when he was found with his head stuck in a barley sack, broke forth into a volume of brag, insisting he had killed seven Indians, and exhibited a piece of salmon skin for a scalp.' Meeker also described Burns as a 'foolhardy Irishman.'

In spite of Matthew's apparent knowledge of Latin, French and Botany, which suggests possible premedical studies, his correspondence with his military superiors reveals an abysmal ignorance of spelling and elementary syntax. On one occasion, his use of 'me' as a possessive pronoun instantly recalls Irish idiom. Furthermore, there are times when one suspects that many of his letters, especially to Shaw and Tilton, were composed and written after copious draughts of medicinal whisky. But much of this correspondence was dispatched from the field, in dangerous, insalubrious conditions, particularly during the winter of 1855–56.

Given the diversity of culture, nationality and race in the Pacific Northwest of the mid-nineteenth century, with substantial numbers of Scots and Irish, it is unlikely that an Irishman would pass as a Scot. The Pierce County Census of 1854[17] lists Burns's entry as '29, Single of CA (California)'. In the 1860 Census of Olympia[13] M. P . Burns, age 34, is stated to be from Scotland, whereas in the Index to the Naturalisation Records for Thurston County, Washington Territory, 1854–1883, revealed a 'Patrick Bruns of Great Britain/Ireland'[18] who sought or was granted naturalisation in 1867. Sadly, despite a thorough search of Thurston County records, the archivists concluded:

> ... that many of the actual naturalization records for early Thurston County did not survive the march of time.[19]

Matthew is not mentioned in the Census of Washington Territory in 1870, nor in that of Thurston County in the same year; neither is he listed in the Records of Deaths in Pierce and Thurston Counties.[20] No other naturalisation or immigration documents that relate to M. P. Burns appear to exist in the California, Oregon, Washington State or National Archives, Washington, D.C.

The evidence that he was Robert's brother rests chiefly on his letter to the 'Governor General of British India'. The date of writing accords with times taken for the international exchange of correspondence in the mid-nineteenth century and Matthew's movements in the Pacific Northwest of the United States. Circumstantial evidence may be adduced from the observations of his peers such as Ezra Meeker, who stated that Matthew was Irish and from the Glasgow *Herald's* report that Robert hailed from Ulster. In the few official documents that survive in Oregon and Washington States, Matthew's birthplace is given severally as Ireland or Scotland. He appears to have been born in 1825 or 1826 and was some two years younger than Robert, who was 'about twenty-seven' when he died in 1851. However, given the narrow variations in their recorded dates of birth, it is possible that they were twins. The brothers, with or without other members of their family, may have left Northern Ireland as teenagers, to join their married sister in Glasgow, after the Census of 1841, but this is conjecture, given the illegibility of some of the surviving records.

The relationship of the Burns Boys to the Bard is at best tenuous. The *Herald* stated that Robert was 'no relation whatever' and according to one of Matthew's contemporaries, the 'Dr.' was heard to say that he was distantly related to the Poet. The clue to their genealogy probably lies in the parish registers of Northern Ireland, but the probability of uncovering the evidence is at best, remote. There are no official records of births and deaths in Ulster before 1864 and migration across the Irish Sea in the nineteenth century was untrammelled by documentation.

Epilogue

St John[1] was in London on Christmas Eve 1866 when he received a telegram from Brooke's friend, Dr Beith, 'an old *Dido* man' who lived in Plymouth. St John had returned from Brooke's home two days earlier, but when he learned that the Raja had suffered another paralytic stroke, he left immediately to be with him. The afternoon express 'flew along through the snow' to reach Plymouth around midnight and after waiting for a carriage, St John and two companions were driven across Dartmoor in the murk of a bleak winter's night. They reached Burrator about 4 a.m. Brooke recovered partially, but was felled by another cerebrovascular attack in June 1868, when he lapsed into coma and died.

Hume, Brooke's long-time adversary in Parliament, predeceased him on 20 February 1855.[2] When he joined the great majority, Hume had served on more committees of the House of Commons than any other member.

Nicol[3] returned to England in 1860, after twenty-eight years in Singapore, to become Chairman of the Chartered Mercantile Bank of India, London and China and a Director of the Eastern Extension, Australasia, and China Telegraph Company, the North British and Mercantile Insurance Company and several other concerns.

He retired to Brighton, in a house overlooking the sea, but removed to Cambridge Gate, Regent's Park, London, probably in the early 1880s. Nicol died on 16 January 1897, fifty years after appointing Burns as an agent of Hamilton, Gray. His will, published in *The Times* the following month,[4] gives the lie in part to this writer's earlier assessment of the man. Nicol, in death, was truly philanthropic. Among many bequests, he left £20,000 to the Provost of Aberdeen for the establishment of the Garden Nicol Benevolent Fund for the aid of distressed gentlewomen, in memory of his mother. A similar amount was donated to the Court of the University of Aberdeen to provide bursaries, scholarships and exhibitions to the English universities for students of that foundation. This was a most enlightened benefaction at that time. The residue of Nicol's estate, considerably in excess of £30,000, provided beds in Aberdeen's three public hospitals and all of the large London teaching hospitals, including the Hospital for Sick Children, Great Ormond Street. Unlike today, these institutions served a large inner city population, many of whom were poor and destitute.

Keppel,[5] by Special Order in Council, remained on the Navy's active list until his death on 17 January 1904. Knight Grand Cross of the Bath and Admiral of the Fleet, Harry Keppel served under four sovereigns, when his intimate friend, the Prince of Wales ascended the throne as Edward VII. His association with Singapore is commemorated in Keppel Dockyard and Keppel Road.

St John[6] survived until 2 January 1910. In 1856, he became British Consul-General in Brunei, where his explorations were later published in 'Life in the Forests of the Far East'. Seven years on, he was Chargé d'Affaires in Haiti and he remained in the Caribbean for twelve years, assuming a similar post in the Dominican Republic in 1871. St John was promoted to Resident Minister in Haiti the following year, before appointment as Minister Residentiary in Peru and Consul-General at Lima. In company with other foreign diplomats, he helped to protect Lima from destruction after Peru's defeat in a war with Chile. St John was knighted in 1881 and assigned to Mexico as Envoy Extraordinary and Minister Plenipotentiary in 1884. His diplomatic career ended in 1896, after three years as Minister to Sweden. He was little mourned, having survived his enemy and close contemporary, Burns, by nearly fifty-nine years. According to Reece,[7] St John's behaviour 'was tempered by an awareness of what he called 'his deficiencies in education and manner'. Many regarded him as a 'cold fish', censorious and humourless to a fault.

Robert Burns was long dead. Matthew disappeared without trace in 1863, although it was said that he continued to practise in the Upper Puget Sound. While the evidence is not compelling, their relationship to the Bard seems, at best, remote. Neither inspired biographies but their lives were far from achromatic. Although they lacked *'Choice words, and measured phrase, above the reach of ordinary men; a stately speech; Such as grave livers do in Scotland use,'* the Burns Boys breathed freedom.

References

Chapter 1: Glasgow

1. *Housing in 19th Century Glasgow*. p.9. City Archivist, Mitchell Library, Glasgow, Scotland.
2. Brooke, J. 'Acceptance of Freedom of City of London'. *Straits Times*, 19 January 1848.
3. Smout, T. C. *A Century of the Scottish People 1830–1950*. p.2. Collins, London, 1986.
   (© 1986, T. C Smout. Permission to quote courtesy of HarperCollins Publishers Ltd)
4. Hutchison, G. and O'Neill, M. *The Springburn Experience*. p.3. Polygon, Edinburgh, 1989.
5. Symons, J. C., 1839. Reports from Assistant Hand-Loom Weavers Commissioners in Gibbs, A. *Glasgow – The Making of a City*. pp. 107–108. Croom Helm, London, 1983.
6. Arnott, N. in Smout, T. C. *A Century of the Scottish People 1830–1950*. p.30.
7. Smout. Ibid. p. 31
8. Supplement to the Registrar-General's Reports on Births, Marriages, and Deaths in Scotland during the ten years 1861–1870. p.53. H.M.S.O. Edinburgh and London, 1874.

Chapter II: James Brooke

1. Farrington, A. A Guide to the Military Department Records. Bengal Service Army Lists. The British Library. Oriental and India Office Collections. Shelfmark: L/Mil/10/24/167/130.
2. St John, S. *The Life of Sir James Brooke, Rajah of Sarawak*. p.2. Oxford University Press, Kuala Lumpur. 1994.
3. Tarling, N. *The Burthen, the Risk, and the Glory*. p.4. Oxford University Press, Kuala Lumpur, 1982.
4. Day, H. *The Norwich School of Painters*. p.9. Eastbourne Fine Art, 1979.
5. Lord Amherst. *National Dictionary of Biography* (ed. L.Stephen and S.Lee) Vol. I. pp. 360–361. Smith Elder, London, 1908.
6. Rutter, O. *Rajah Brooke and Baroness Burdett Coutts*. pp. 18–19. Hutchinson, London, 1935.
7. Sylvia, Lady Brooke. *Queen of the Head-hunters*. p.134. Oxford University Press, Kuala Lumpur, 1993.
8. Larn, R. and B. *Shipwreck Index of the British Isles*. Vol. 2, Section 2. Lloyd's Register of Shipping, London, 1995.
9. St John, *Sir James Brooke*, p. vi.
10. Jacob, G. L. *The Rajah of Sarawak*. Vol. I. pp. 26–27. Macmillan, London, 1876.
11. Mundy, R. *Narrative of Events in Borneo and Celebes*. Vol. I. pp. 6–8. Murray, London, 1848.

Chapter III: Brooke, Raja of Sarawak

1. Brooke, J. in J. C. Templer, ed. *The Private Letters of Sir James Brooke, K.C.B.* Vol. I. p. 22. Bentley, London, 1853.
2. Rutter, O. *Rajah Brooke and Baroness Burdett Coutts*. pp. 24–25. Hutchinson, London, 1935.
3. Mundy, R. *Narrative of Events*. Vol. I. p.12.
4. Brooke to Templer, 3 June 1839. *Private Letters*. Vol. I. p.53.
5. Ibid. 18 June 1839. p. 55.
6. Ibid. 20 August 1839. p. 66.

7. Keppel, H. *The Expedition to Borneo of H.M.S. Dido for the Suppression of Piracy*. Vol. I. pp. 74–75. Chapman and Hall, 1847.
8. Ibid. p. 171.
9. Ibid. p. 210.
10. Ibid. p. 213.
11. Brooke to Templer, 25 September 1841. *Private Letters*. Vol. I. p. 115.
12. Mundy, R. *Narrative of Events*. Vol. I. pp. 344–345.
13. Keppel, *Dido*. Vol. II. p. 67.

Chapter IV: Borneo

1. Omar, A. H. *The Malay Peoples of Malaysia and their Languages*. pp. 14–25. Dewan Bahasa dan Pustaka Kementarian Pelajaran Malaysia. Kuala Lumpur, 1983.
2. Rutter, O. *British North Borneo. An Account of its History, Resources and Native Tribes*. p. 4. Constable, London, 1922.
3. Omar, pp. 37–41.
4. Roth, H. L. *The Natives of Sarawak and British North Borneo*. Vol. I. pp. 39–43. University of Malaya Press, Kuala Lumpur, 1968.
5. Omar, p. 30.
6. Low, H. *Sarawak; its inhabitants and productions*. p. 30. Bentley, London, 1848.
7. Keppel, *Dido*, Vol. II. p. 2.

Chapter V: Sir James Brooke

1. St John, *Sir James Brooke*. pp. 124–125.
2. Ibid. p. 125.
3. Oxford University Archives, Bodleian Library, University of Oxford.
4 St John, *Sir James Brooke*. pp. 126–128.
5. Keppel, H. *A Sailor's Life Under Four Sovereigns*. Vol. II. p. 62. Macmillan, London, 1899.
6. St John, *Sir James Brooke*. p. 129.
7. Ibid. p. 131.
8. Keppel, *A Sailor's Life*. Vol. II. p. 70.
9. Ibid. p. 73.
10. St John, *Sir James Brooke*. p. 133.
11. Ibid. p. 136.
12. Brooke to Templer, 12 November 1839. *Private Letters*. Vol. I. p. 80.
13. Brooke to Mrs Brooke, 16 March 1842. Ibid. p. 184.
14. *Singapore Free Press*, 24 August 1848.

Chapter VI: Burns and Old Singapore

1. Clyde Bill of Entry and Shipping List. Vol. V, No. 73, Thursday June 18th, 1846. Custom-House, Glasgow.
2. 'Black Ball' Line of British and Australian Ex-Royal Mail Packets. Merseyside Maritime Museum, Liverpool.
3. 'Black Ball' and 'Eagle Line'. Ibid.
4. *Straits Times*, 28 October 1846.
5. *Sydney Shipping Gazette and Sydney General Trade List*. p. 65. 10 March 1849.
6. *Straits Times*, 12 August 1845.
7. Buckley, C. B. *An Anecdotal History of Old Times in Singapore*. p. 64. University of Malaya Press, Kuala Lumpur, 1965.
8. *Straits Times*, 14 November 1846.

9. *Singapore Free Press*, 31 May 1849.
10. *Straits Times*, 29 April 1850.
11. Ibid. 30 December 1846.
12. *Singapore Free Press*, 29 June 1848.
13. Creighton, C. *History of Epidemics in Britain A.D. 1666–1893*. Vol. II. pp. 835–839. Cambridge University Press, 1894.
14. *Punch*, 13, 6–2, p. 168. London, 1847.

Chapter VII: Antimony, Burns and Brooke

1. Buckley, *Anecdotal History*, pp. 398–399.
2. Ibid. p. 453.
3. The Late Mr G. G. Nicol. *Singapore Free Press*, 16 February 1897.
4. *Straits Times*, 1 January 1847.
5. Burns, R. *Journal of the Indian Archipelago and Eastern Asia*. Vol. II. p. 152. Singapore, 1849.
6. *Singapore Free Press*, 30 September 1847.
7. Ibid. 21 October 1847.
8. Crookshank to Chiefs of Bintulu, 5 January 1848. HC Sessional Papers 1852–53, LXI, p. 347.
9. Gliddon and Co. to Rear-Admiral Inglefield, 7 December 1847. PRO. CO. 144/2.
10. Memorial of the Chamber of Commerce of Glasgow. 3 February 1848. HC Sessional Papers 1851, XXXV, [1375] pp. 11–12.
11. Burns to Nicol, 14 February 1848. *Singapore Free Press*, 28 May 1852.
12. Nicol to Burns, 7 March 1848. Ibid.
13. Ibid. 17 March 1848.
14. Ibid. 15 May 1848.
15. Buchanan to President of Board of Trade, 6 March 1848. *Singapore Free Press*, 25 May 1848.
16. Committee of Privy Council for Trade to Buchanan, 13 March 1848. Archives of Glasgow Chamber of Commerce, Mitchell Library, Glasgow, Scotland.

Chapter VIII: The best laid schemes ...

1. Brooke to Palmerston, 31 May 1848. HC Sessional Papers 1852, XXXI, pp. 13–14.
2. Brooke to Stanley, 31 May 1848. Ibid. p. 14.
3. Brooke to Kinnear, 26 May 1848. Ibid. pp. 15–16.
4. Nicol to Burns, 5 June 1848. *Singapore Free Press*, 28 May 1848.
5. Nicol to Burns, 9 June 1848. Ibid.
6.` Nicol to Burns, 30 June 1848. Ibid.
7. Nicol to Burns, 23 July 1848. Ibid.
8. Nicol to Burns, 28 August 1848. Ibid.
9. Burns to Nicol, 4 September 1848. Ibid.
10. Burns to Nicol, 26 September 1848. Ibid.
11. Nicol to Burns, 1 November 1848. Ibid.

Chapter IX: Burns, Explorer and Ethnographer

1. Burns, R. *Journal of the Indian Archipelago and Eastern Asia*. Vol. II. pp. 140–152. February 1849.
2. Burns, ibid. Vol. III. pp. 182–192, March 1849.

3.   Editor, ibid. Vol. II. pp. 138–139, February 1849.
4.   Low, *Sarawak*, pp. 333–334.
5.   Harrisson, T. *The Sarawak Museum Journal*. Vol. V No. 3, pp. 463–494, Kuching, 1951.
6.   Buckley, *Anecdotal History*, p. 487.
7.   Brooke to Templer, 26 November 1848. *Private Letters*, Vol. II, pp. 230–231.
8.   Burns to Nicol, 5 November 1848. *Singapore Free Press*, 28 May 1852.
9.   *Straits Times*, 4 November 1848.
10. Ibid. 2 December 1848.

Chapter X: Burns, the Sultan and Brooke

1.   Minutes of a Conversation between Mr Low and the Pangeran Makota. 11 January 1849. HC Sessional Papers 1852, XXXI, pp. 546–548.
2.   Ibid. p. 548.
3.   Sultan of Bruné to Brooke, 9-Rabi-al-awal, 1266 (1849). Ibid. p. 548.
4.   Burns to Brooke, 18 June 1849. Ibid. p. 456.
5.   Grant to Burns, 18 June 1849. Ibid. p. 457.
6.   Burns to Brooke, 19 June 1849. Ibid. p. 455–456.
7.   Grant to Burns, 20 June 1849. p. 456.
8.   Brooke in Keppel, H. *A Visit to the Indian Archipelago in H.M. Ship Maeander*. Vol. II. p. 89. Richard Bentley, London, MDCCCLIII.
9.   *Straits Times*, 29 January 1850.
10. *Singapore Free Press*, 2 April 1850.
11. Brooke to Burns, 28 July 1850. HC Sessional Papers, 1852, XXXI, p. 455.
12. Award of Sir James Brooke. 24 December 1850. Ibid. p. 455.
13. Brooke to Palmerston, 28 December 1850. Ibid. p. 452.
14. Rajahs of Barram to Mr Scott and Mr Low. Ibid. p. 454.

Chapter XI: Maludu Bay

1.   *Straits Times*, 20 May 1851.
2.   Burns to Palmerston, 28 June 1851. HC Sessional Papers 1852–53, XXXI, pp. 447–449
3.   *North British Daily Mail*, 6 October 1851.
4.   Ibid. 7 October 1851.
5.   *Singapore Free Press* (Overland Edition), 6 October 1851.
6.   *Straits Times*, 22 July 1851.
7.   Deposition of Karnoor, 2 December 1851. HC Sessional Papers 1852–53, LXI, pp. 249–250.

Chapter XII: The Amok

1.   Low, *Sarawak*, p. 129.
2.   *Straits Times*, 2 December 1851.
3.   St John to Rear-Admiral Austen, 25 November 1851. HC Sessional Papers 1852–53, LXI, p. 236.
4.   *Straits Times*, 2 December 1851.
5.   *Singapore Free Press*, 28 February 1852.
6.   *Straits Times*, 9 December 1851.
7.   St John, S. *Life in the Forests of the Far East*. Vol. II, pp. 222–232. Oxford University Press, Kuala Lumpur, 1974.

8.   St John, *Sir James Brooke*, p. 239.

Chapter XIII: The *Dolphin* Avenged

1.   Massie to Church, 10 December 1851. HC Sessional Papers 1852–53, LXI, p. 247.
2.   Blundell to Massie, 22 December 1851. Ref. 7760, 1851. pp. 263–266. Index to Straits Settlements Records. Series A–Z 1800–1875, Singapore National Archives.
3.   Austen to Massie, 29 December 1851. HC Sessional Papers 1852–53, LXI pp. 238–239.
4.   Massie to Austen, 19 February 1852. Ibid. pp. 241–242.
5.   Cecil, D. *A Portrait of Jane Austen.* p. 200. Constable, London, 1978.

Chapter XIV: ' And ev'n his failings lean'd to Virtue's side.'

1.   Hume, J. *The Medical Directory for Scotland. 1856.* pp. 151–153. Churchill, London.
2.   Personal Communication. 12 August 1997. Archivist, Royal College of Surgeons, Edinburgh.
3.   St John, Sir James Brooke. p. 236.
4.   Brooke to Templer, 16 September 1848. *Private Letters.* Vol. II, pp. 224–225.
5.   Hume to Palmerston, 20 December 1851. HC Sessional Papers 1852, XXXI, p. 457.
6.   Gliddon to Hume, 25 November 1851. Ibid. pp. 457–459.
7.   Crookshank to Chiefs of Bintulu, 5 January 1848. HC Sessional Papers 1852–53, LXI, p. 347.

Chapter XV: 'Intrigues, half-gather'd, conversation-scraps … '

1.   Hume to Malmesbury. 7 April 1852. HC Sessional Papers 1852, XXXI, pp. 476–481.
2.   Tarling, N. *The Burthen, the Risk, and the Glory.* p. 123. Oxford University Press, Kuala Lumpur, 1982.
3.   Correspondence Relative to the Removal of Mr W. Napier, Lt.-Governor of Labuan. HC Sessional Papers 1851, XXXI, p. 133.
4.   St John to Brooke, 22 April 1852. Ibid. 1852/53. LXI, pp. 348–349.
5.   Brooke to Malmesbury, 11 October 1852. Ibid. pp. 354–355.
6.   Brooke to Sultan of Borneo et al, Undated. Ibid. pp. 355–356.
7.   Sultan of Borneo et al. to Brooke, 11 Ramdan. Ibid. p. 356.
8.   Brooke to Granville, 5 January 1852. Ibid. pp. 460–462.
9.   Ibid., 24 January 1852. Ibid. pp. 462.
10. Makota to Brooke, 28 Zul-Hadji (no year stated). Ibid. p. 463.
11. Brooke to Granville, 12 February 1852. Ibid. p. 463.
12. Inclosure 1 in No. 9. Hamilton to Bouverie, 8 February 1852. Ibid. p. 463.
13. Inclosure 2 in No. 9. Aplin to Brooke, 28 January 1852. Ibid. p. 464.
14. Brooke to Granville, 19 February 1852. Ibid. pp. 465–466.

Chapter XVI: 'Nature's law … '

1.   Grimble, I. *The Trial of Patrick Sellar.* p. iii. Routledge and Kegan Paul, London, 1962.
2.   *The Times* (London), 20 May 1845.

Chapter XVII: The Search for Burns

1.   Personal Communication. 28 December 1995. Nellie Dato Paduka Haji Sunny, Dewan

Bahasa dan Pustaka Brunei, Bandar Seri Begawan 2064, Brunei, Darussalam.
2. Ibid. 23 February 1995. J. Jamieson, Dunfermline Carnegie Library, Scotland.
3. M'Naught, D. *The Burns Chronicle and Club Directory*. Vol. III, pp. 90–95, 1894.
4. Ibid. Vol. IV, pp. 76–89, 1895.
5. M'Millan, W. Ibid. Vol. XXXIV, pp. 35–38, 1925.
6. Mackay, J. *Burns – A Biography of Robert Burns*. pp. 425–426. Headline Book Publishing Company plc, London, 1993.
7. Personal Communication. 1 September 1997. G. Pick, London Metropolitan Archives.
8. Mathijsen, M. *De brieven van De Schoolmeester*. Em. Querido's Uitgeverij, b.v., Amsterdam, 1987.
9. King, V. T. and Talib, N.S. in *Explorers of South-East Asia* (ed. King, V.T.) pp. 161–162. Oxford University Press, Kuala Lumpur, 1995.
10. Branigan, D. P. *The Scots Magazine*, Vol. V, No. 3, pp. 584–591, 1975.
11. Harrisson, T. *The Sarawak Museum Journal*, Vol. V, No. 3, pp. 463–494, Kuching, 1951.
12 Personal Communication. 1 July 1996. J. Currie, Special Collections, Edinburgh University Library, Scotland.
13. *Straits Times*, 18 May 1852.
14. Burns, M. P. to Governor General of British India, 5 May 1853. S/No. 6265 Ref. S20, 1853. Index to Straits Settlements Records. Series A–Z 1800–1875, Singapore National Archives.

Chapter XVIII: M. P. Burns

1. Blundell, E. A. to Couper, G., 6 October 1853. Index to Straits Settlements Records Series A–Z 1800–1875, Singapore National Archives.
2. Personal communication. 24 September 1997. T. Backer, Oregon State Archives, Salem, Oregon, USA.
3. *Frontier Justice. Guide to Court Records of Washington Territory 1853–1889* Office of the Secretary of State, Olympia, Washington, January 1987. THR–127 Case #125, 1854. Plaintiff: Territory of Washington.
4. Ibid. PRC-260 Case #251, 1855. Plaintiff: Swindle, W. Charles.
5. Ibid. THR-232 Case #231, 1859. Plaintiff: Miles, Morrill, Charles.
6. Ibid. THR-284 Case# 282 1/2, Plaintiff: Miles, William E.; Pray, James B.: Miles and Pray.
7. Census of Olympia, Thurston County, WA Territory, Washington State Archives, Olympia, WA, U.S.A.
8. Washington State Archives, SW Regional Branch, Thurston County Deed, Vol. 3, p. 28.
9. Ibid. Vol. 4, p. 246.

Chapter XIX: Matthew Burns M.D.

1. Scott, H. W. *History of the Oregon Country* (compiled by L. M. Scott). Vol. II, Chapt. XVI, p. 36.Riverside Press, Cambridge, MA, USA, 1924.
2. Muster Rolls of the Washington Territorial Volunteers. Washington State Archives, WA, USA.
3. Prosch, C. *Reminiscences of Washington Territory*, pp. 85–86. Ye Galleon Press, Fairfield, Washington, 1969.

Chapter XX: Matthew Burns — Regimental Surgeon

1. Muster Rolls of the Washington Territorial Volunteers. Territorial Papers, Washington State Archives.

2. Rabbeson, A. B. to Editor, *Pioneer and Democrat*, 9 November 1855.
3. Meeker, E. *The Tragedy of Leschi*. Republished by the Historical Society of Seattle and King County, Washington State, 1980.
4. Ibid. *Pioneer Reminiscences of Puget Sound*. Lowman and Hanford, Seattle, WA, 1905.
5. Nugent to Tilton. 2 November 1855. Territorial Papers.
6. Burnes to Tilton, Pioneer and Democrat, 2 November 1855.
7. Lodge to Editor, 9 November 1855, ibid.
8. Burns to Tilton, 24 January 1856. Territorial Papers.
9. Burns to Stevens, 12 February 1856. Ibid.
10. Burns to Tilton, 16 February 1856. Ibid.
11. Tilton to Burns, 18 February 1856. Ibid.
12. Burns to Tilton, 23 February 1856. Ibid.
13. Burns to Stevens, 28 February 1856. Ibid.
14. Burns to Steven. Ibid.
15. Burns to Tilton, 29 February 1856. Ibid.
16. Tilton to Burns, 2 March 1856. Ibid.
17. Burns to Tilton, 11 March 1856. Ibid.
18. Burns to Tilton, 24 March 1856. Ibid.
19. Tilton to Burns, 27 March 1856. Ibid.
20. Tilton to Burns. Ibid.
21. Burns to Miller, undated. Ibid.
22. Burns to Acting Quartermaster, Fort Montgomery. *Seattle Times*, 15 January 1956.
23. Burns to Stevens, 2 April 1856. Territorial Volunteer Papers.
24. Burns to Stevens, 9 April 1856. Ibid.
25. Ibid. 26 April 1856. Ibid.
26. Burns to Tilton, 29 April 1856. Ibid.
27. Burns to Tilton. Ibid.
28. Tilton to Burns, 1 May 1856. Ibid.
29. Burns to Shaw, 21 May 1856. Ibid.
30. Tilton to Shaw, 21 May 1856. Ibid.
31. Tilton to Maxon, 29 May 1856. Ibid.
32. Burns to Tilton, 12 July 1856. Ibid.
33. W. M. Rifles to Shaw, 12 July 1856. Ibid.
34. *An Illustrated History of Klickitat, Yakima and Kittitas Counties*. Pp. 82–83. Interstate Publishing Company, 1904.
35. List of Articles Captured by Dr Burns on Grande Ronde. 1 July 1856. Territorial Volunteer Papers.
36. Burns to Robie, 24 July 1856. Ibid.
37. Burns to Stevens, 31 July 1856. Ibid.
38. Burns to Shaw, 14 August 1856. Ibid.
39. Burns to Tilton, 24 August 1856. Ibid.
40. Burns to Stevens, 18 September 1856. Ibid.
41. *Pioneer and Democrat*, 5 June 1857.
42. Ibid. 19 June 1857.

Chapter XXI: 'Who can be ... temperate and furious ... in a moment? No man.'

1. Buckley, *Anecdotal History*, p. 425.
2. Ibid. p. 471.
3. Ibid. p. 406.
4. Nicol to Brooke, 30 March 1852. HC Sessional Papers 1852. XXXI, pp. 545–546.

5. Burns to Nicol, 14 February 1848. *Singapore Free Press*, 28 May 1852.
6. Harrisson, T. *The Sarawak Museum Journal*. Vol. V, No. 3, pp. 463–494. Kuching, 1951.
7. Irwin, G. *Nineteenth Century Borneo. A Study in Diplomatic Rivalry*. p. 131. Donald Moore Books, Singapore, 1967.

Chapter XXII: 'You shall seek all day ere you find them.'

1. Personal communication. 12 February 1999. Ulster Historical Foundation, Belfast.
2. Ibid. 5 December 1997. Archivist, Royal College of Physicians and Surgeons, Glasgow.
3. Ibid. 8 October 1997. Special Collections, Edinburgh University Library.
4. Ibid. 13 October 1997. Keeper of Manuscripts and Muniments, University of St Andrews Library.
5. Ibid. 10 November 1997. Archivist, Archives and Business Records Centre, University of Glasgow.
6. Ibid. 10 October 1997. University Archives, University of Strathclyde.
7. Ibid. 20 October, 1997. Directorate of Information Systems and Services, Library Division, Department of Special Collections and Archives, University of Aberdeen.
8. Ibid. 13 September 1997. Stephen Greenberg, History of Medicine Division, National Library of Medicine, National Institutes of Health, Bethesda, MD, USA.
9. Ibid. 3 November 1997. Librarian, Royal College of Physicians of Edinburgh.
10. Ibid. 27 October 1998. Archivist, Medical Quality Assurance Commission, Department of Health, Washington State, USA
11. Medical Records of East India Company 1840–1853. British Medical Association Library, London.
12. Crawford, D. G. *Roll of the Indian Medical Service 1615–1930*. Thacker and Co., London, 1930.
13. Census of Olympia, Thurston County, WA Territory, Washington State Archives, Olympia, WA, USA.
14. Muster Rolls of the Washington Territorial Volunteers. Territorial Volunteer Papers, Washington State Archives.
15. Scott, H. W. *History of the Oregon Country* (compiled by L. M. Scott). Vol. II, p. 41. Riverside Press, Cambridge, MA, USA.
16. Meeker, E. Pioneer Reminiscences of Puget Sound. Lowman and Hanford, Seattle, WA, USA, 1905.
17. Pierce County Census, 1854. Card Index #226, Seattle Public Library, WA, USA.
18. Index to the Naturalisation Journal 1854–1883. Washington State Archives.
19. Personal Communication. 30 July 1998. Archives and Records Management Division, Washington State Archives.
20. Personal Communication. 9 December 1997. Maxine Day Alexander, Tacoma, WA, USA.

Epilogue

1. St John, Sir James Brooke, pp. 375–376.
2. Hume, J. Dictionary of National Biography. S. Lee, ed. Vol. X, pp. 230–231. Smith Elder, London, 1908.
3. Personal Communication, 15 April 1998. D. Hedgecock, Guildhall Library, London.
4. The Times (London), 8 February 1897.
5. Keppel, H. Dictionary of National Biography. S. Lee, ed. Second Suppl. 1901–1911. Vol. II, pp. 393–394. Reprinted by Oxford University Press, London, 1920.
6. St John, S. Ibid. Vol. III, pp. 249–250.
7. Reece, R. H. W. in Introduction to St John, S. Life of Sir James Brooke, pp. vii–l.

Glossary

Baba	descendant of earliest Chinese settlers in the Straits of Malacca
Cutter	a single–masted boat rigged like a sloop e.g. *Young Frederick* sailed by Burns on some of his trading ventures
Datu, Datuk, Dato	non-royal title of distinction
Godown	warehouse or store
Jangan lawan!	don't fight!
Jolly-boat	small, clinker-built boat usually hoisted on a davit at the ship's stern
Jurumudi	steersman or quartermaster
Jury-rig	temporary or makeshift sails, spars and tackle to bring a disabled ship to harbour e.g. *Royalist*
Kati, catty	a unit of weight equivalent to one and one-third pounds
Kris	Malay dagger with sinuous, double-edged blade
Lari!	Run!
Lascar	East-Indian seaman in this text
Nakhoda	captain or master of native trading vessel
Orang kaya	title given to highest dignitaries
Pangeran	prince, noble
Perahu	undecked native vessel
Scandalize	reduce the area of a sail by lowering the peak and hauling up the tack
Serang	head lascar
Spanker	fore and aft sail set with gaff and boom, abaft the after mast on a sailing ship
Sumpitan	blowpipe
Sundang	Sulu swordkris. A heavy cutting two-edged weapon with a cockatoo hilt
Supercargo	abbreviation of cargo-superintendent; representative of the ship's owner responsible for commercial dealings involving ship and cargo
Towkay	Chinese man of substance
Tuan besar	a great lord, a man of standing

Cualann Press Titles

Scotland and the Cold War
Editor: Brian P. Jamison
ISBN 0 9544416 1 3 ... Price £12.99 (p/b 192, illustrated)

Gurkha Reiver
Neil Griffiths
ISBN 0 9544416 0 5 ... Price £10.99 (p/b 192, illustrated)

Full Circle: Log of the Navy's No. 1 Conscript
John Gritten
Foreword: Dr Peter Liddle, Director, The Second World War Experience Centre, Leeds
ISBN 0 9535036 9 0 ... Price £19.99 (Hardback, 352 pages, illustrated)

In Search of Willie Patterson: A Scottish Soldier in the Age of Imperialism
Dr Fred Reid
Foreword: Prof W Hamish Fraser, University of Strathclyde
ISBN 0 9535036 7 4 ... Price £10.99 (p/b 160 pages, illustrated)

The Lion and the Eagle: Reminiscences of Polish Second World War Veterans in Scotland
Editor: Dr Diana M Henderson LLB TD FSA Scot.
Foreword: His Excellency Dr Stanislaw Komorowski
ISBN: 0 9535036 4 X ... £9.99 (p/b 160 pages, illustrated)

Stand By Your Beds! A Wry Look at National Service
David Findlay Clark OBE, MA, Ph.D., C.Psychol., F.B.Ps.S.
Preface: Trevor Royle, historian and writer
ISBN: 0 9535036 6 6 ... £13.99 (p/b 256 pages, illustrated)

Open Road to Faraway: Escapes from Nazi POW Camps 1941-1945
Andrew Winton D A (Edin)
Foreword: Allan Carswell, National War Museum of Scotland
ISBN: 0 9535036 5 8 ... £9.99 (p/b 160 pages, illustrated)

Beyond the Bamboo Screen: Scottish Prisoners of War under the Japanese
Tom McGowran OBE.
Foreword and Illustrations by G S Gimson QC
ISBN 0 9535036 1 5 ... Price £9.99 (p/b 160 pages, illustrated)

On Flows the Tay: Perth and the First World War
Dr Bill Harding Ph.D., FEIS
Foreword: Alan Hamilton, *The Times* journalist and author
ISBN 0 9535036 2 3 ... Price £12.99 (p/b 192 pages, illustrated)

Of Fish and Men: Tales of a Scottish Fisher
David C Watson.
Foreword: Derek Mills
ISBN 0 9535036 3 1 ... Price £10.99 (p/b 160 pages, illustrated)

Coasting around Scotland
Nicholas Fairweather
Foreword: Robin Harper MSP
ISBN 0 9535036 8 2 ... Price £12.99 (p/b 200 pages, b/w and colour photos)